# HOW I MADE
# ONE MILLION DOLLARS
# ...LAST YEAR
# ...TRADING COMMODITIES

by
Larry R. Williams

Windsor Books, Brightwaters, N.Y.

Published by Windsor Books
P.O. Box 280
Brightwaters, N.Y. 11718

ISBN 0-930233-10-7

**THIRD EDITION**

**CAVEAT:** It should be noted that all commodities trades, patterns, charts, systems, etc., discussed in this book are for illustrative purposes only and are not to be construed as specific advisory recommendations. Further note that no method of trading or investing is foolproof or without difficulty, and past performance is no guarantee of future performance. All ideas and material presented are entirely those of the author and do not necessarily reflect those of the publisher or bookseller.

The value of this book seems best expressed, not in the hundreds of complimentary letters but in the fact it is now in its second printing in English and first printing in the German language.

What's in store for you is an overall view of the markets, how I made money, the tools and techniques. The events described herein took place in 1973 . . . the year of a big bull market. But that does not matter — the tools were developed before 1973 and will work long after traders have stopped talking about that spectacular year.

As one who has had major ups and downs, in the market and his own personal life, I want to share this one thought with you: It is that we must not refrain from life, rather we must give ourselves to it . . . fully . . . keeping in mind that a good life is far more valuable than the best trade you will ever make.

Winter arrives only if you allow it.

LARRY WILLIAMS

A SPECIAL NOTE OF THANKS
All daily market charts shown to illustrate Mr. Williams' techniques are shown through the courtesy of Commodity Research Bureau, One Liberty Plaza, New York City, New York 10006. Their charts and books are a must for all commodity traders.

# TABLE OF CONTENTS

## CHAPTER ELEVEN

CHAPTER ONE

EXACTLY HOW I MADE MY MILLION DOLLARS

# CHAPTER ONE

## EXACTLY HOW I MADE MY MILLION DOLLARS

Surely, every speculator dreams of making a million dollars or more in the brief time period of one year. Unfortunately, few of us accomplish this seemingly impossible dream. As one who has done just that, I'd like to tell you how it was accomplished. And further more, I'm going to tell you what I'll do differently the next time I try!

There have been several other books on how to make millions in the stock market. While they do make interesting reading, (possibly even more entertaining than this bit of writing) I felt the books did not really tell the reader exactly how to get out and make that money. All the book buyer was receiving was an interesting story but none of the tools or concepts that would enable him to meet with similar success.

It has also been my belief that a truly good, educational book should, in all likelihood, be a rather small one. Perhaps the old adage that "good things come in small packages" could apply here. Or, perhaps it's just that a truly great idea can be succinctly stated. I prefer to think it is the latter.

In my personal collection of market books, (and I have books ranging in value from $1.00 to $5,000) the smaller books, for some strange reason, are always the best. The stock market courses with their thousands of pages, millions of words, illustrations (and in some cases, even casette tape recordings) seem to miss the mark.

Perhaps the answer lies in the fact that anyone busy enough to have made a million dollars just doesn't have the time to fool around filling up blank pages. The fellow who's not quite as successful, seems to have a bit more time on his hands.

In any event, this is certainly not a big book by any standards. It is, however, an accurate account of how I made over one million dollars in the 1973 commodity market. It is, in essence, the anatomy of a "killing", executed by a well-defined plan of action rather than a joy-ride on lady luck's bandwagon. All of my well-used tools are described herein along with the underlying concepts.

As important as these tools and concepts may be (and you can't succeed without them) I'm inclined to feel that the most vital factors in market success are of a personal nature. They are vision, diligence and perserverance.

My wife says I'm too goal oriented. That I see everything in terms of goals, levels and plateaus. Perhaps so. But this does seem to be a very successful way of "skinning the cat." At least it has been for me. Certainly, if you do not have the vision that you can succeed, you just aren't going to make it. After all, if you're going to dream — why not dream BIG? I advise you to establish high goals and then expand upon them.

A few short years ago I never "dreamed" I would make a million dollars in one year. And . . . I didn't.

One of the strongest motivating factors for me is my ego-involvement with the market and other traders. While the money is nice, I find it even more rewarding to know that I have, and will continue, to beat the market.

However, too much of a good thing can sometimes have its ill effect. Especially when the ego is involved. Ego-tripping can, all too easily, push you into arguing with the market or making risky trades in an effort to prove your brilliance. Ego-tripping can also force you to call the exact high and low of each move. Such an approach dooms you to failure. The markets are very, very difficult. They demand all of our attention and energies. By their very nature, they drain our electrical reserves to the point of coercing us to do things we should not.

## HOW DREAMS COME TRUE

One thing I can state unequivocally: If you don't have any money to invest in the market, you'll never make your million! Many readers of my book on the stock market seem to think that all it takes is a good system and the money will come from heaven. Maybe so! It certainly didn't work that way for me! As a matter of fact, when I was giving stock market seminars throughout the country, some people would try to gain entrance without paying the nominal $30.00 fee simply because they didn't have that kind of money. How incredible! It stands to reason; if you are in the market, you already have the money. If you want to get into the market and don't have the money, you'd better find a way to get the cash.

To an extent, this is what I did. In the fall of 1972 I began forming limited partnerships. That is, people came to see me asking me to manage their accounts. In some cases there were seven people in each partnership. In others there were nine. As general partner, I had complete discretion with the accounts. Realistically speaking, the money was mine to do with as I saw fit. In total, some $300,000 was presented to me for management. This meant I had a decent interest in a large amount of money but my own financial involvement was limited. I had less than $3,000 invested in the $300,000 but I was also contributing my skills and market abilities to the partners. This is one way you can acquire the necessary funds to correctly trade the markets. Prove, in your own limited account, that you can make money in the market and you will be able to attract additional money to manage. Make certain, however, that you comply with local and federal requirements to do this.

2

Should you wish to do it strictly on your own shoestring (which is a more conventional method) I suggest you save your money until you have at least $10,000. Ideally, you should have $20,000. Once this has been attained you can commence trading in a professional manner.

After you have acquired the bankroll, it's time to select the proper tools. That's why you bought this book and my main reason for writing. The tools you will learn are technical and fundamental. The technical tools, by themselves, will be of little value. The same for the fundamental tools. It is only by combining the two that I have been able to meet with market success. By and large, the fundamental indices will serve to select the commodities most likely to have large up or down moves. The technical data will help you decide when to get in and out of those special situations that have been ferreted out by the fundamentals.

To arbitrarily trade any commodity with my technical tools is a mistake. It will not work for me or you. The tools will work only for futures that you have pre-screened and qualified as potential "sure-thing" trades. The importance of this cannot be overlooked. There is no one perfect trading tool or system. Systems only work when they are based on valid, underlying truths. Trading systems, usually based on price change or price trend, will be useless in trading range markets. Buy signals will spell disaster in bear markets, etc.

For this reason, you must first select the one or two commodities that have heavy odds in their favor — then apply the technical tools.

Along with a good set of tools, you will need dedication to your calling. Without dedication you will fail to do your work at the times you should be working.

To my knowledge, there is no other occupation more demanding and trying than speculation. If you are to follow the markets, if you are to see your dream become a reality, you must be on your toes at all times. You must give a good deal of yourself to that dream and you must follow the markets on a daily basis.

## LADY LUCK — DOES SHE EXIST?

I would be remiss in thinking that my success is not based, in part, on just a nice rendezvous with Lady Luck. In fact, you might speculate that my killing in the market was based on nothing more than a lucky stroke of her wand. You know, being in the right place — a bull market — at the right time.

As I write this chapter, I am becoming acutely aware that the possibility does exist since the market has been very hard on me the past three weeks. It's been darned near impossible to make a decent trade. At times like this, one is very tempted to postulate that past successes were based more on luck than skill. However, if one assumes such a defeatist attitude, he will not be able to come back and get on the right side of things again.

If luck has played any part in my success it's been the luck (or privilege, if you will) of associating with some very warm, admirable people; my secretary, Janice, my consultant, Bill Meehan and Lee Turnbull. It's also been rewarding, personally, to have a very good broker, Al Alasandra, who has seen me through the good and bad times.

In the final analysis of life I have come to the conclusion all that really matters are people and nature. People who can love and understand at the same time. These are the things that really count when we grow old and the world continues to revolve past and beyond us.

Most of the partners (not all of them) whose money I have been managing are really tremendous people. They are, for the most part, the kind of people who are out-and-out winners in their everyday lives. They appreciate the fact that any undue pressure on their advisor will only burden him and make his decisions that much more difficult to arrive at.

Stay away from negative people — losers and the fast buck artists. Allign yourself only with the best people and the best firms whether you are going after a $10,000 killing or a $1,000,000 jackpot.


## WHAT I WOULD DO DIFFERENTLY

Past performance is no assurance of future results. However, if we take the time to observe our errors, an analysis of the past can assuredly help us improve upon our future performance.

In looking back over the past twelve months I can spot a number of mistakes. And, I suspect, if I make these errors, so does everyone else.

My number one error has always been that I do not focus enough on the "loaded trades." For one reason or another I find myself straying into marginal, or even bad trades. I do not know why I do it . . . only that it happens.

A helpful solution for me is writing down, on a piece of paper, my reason for making that trade. Once the reasons are there, in black and white, I can quickly see if I'm crap shooting or about to enter a loaded situation.

There are mediocre trades presented every day, but there are only a very few sure-thing trades. We tend to overlook the best trades. You cannot allow this to happen to you if you are going to succeed in commodities. The high risk trades will nickle and dime you to death. The only big money I've ever made has been earned by sitting tight on good positions. In and out trading does little more than pay the broker, it usually loses money for me. You must stay with red hot trades. Forget about day trading, about trying to scalp a few points or about selling for a reaction in a bull market.

One fellow I know had good vision in the Plywood market in late 1972 when it staged a dynamic rally. He knew it would go much higher. However, along the way he decided that it was time for a small pullback. Accordingly, he sold out his long positions and shorted an equal amount.

It was a good decision because prices did begin to pull back and for a few days he showed a profit.

Then, without warning, prices began limiting up, seven days in a row. Before my friend could get out of the market he had lost $62,000. His error was in looking for too small a move and overlooking the big move.

So-so trades that offer a possible gain equal to, or only slightly greater than the risk, must eventually drag all traders down. Regardless of how agile or smart you are, if you play around with these dangerous situations, you will be hurt.

I know!

Another thing I've learned is to pay closer attention to the market and use more discipline in my own trading. Perhaps this example will best illustrate what I mean.

A few days ago I took down a small position of Wheat for a trading turn. The risk/reward ratio was good. Fortunately, it immediately popped up the limit. I had a nice profit and prices closed up limit for the day. Equally important was that the day's activity came at a time when a bottom was projected (and had all the appearances of being a bottom day) because prices were down limit early in the session and then snapped back.

The following morning the indications from the floor were that prices would open substantially higher . . . that there was a good deal of strong buy orders on the floor. I was all set for a nice trade.

But, in the event something was to go wrong I felt it would be indicated by prices opening weak rather than strong. I told myself that if that did happen I should exit the trade and stand aside.

5

Well, prices did open weak. Instead of being up substantially, they were off to unchanged. That was my sell indication.

Did I sell? No, I waited. Waited for something . . . some kind of bounce or burst in prices to the upside (despite the fact that I had my selling indication). In the first five minutes of trading I should have been liquidating the position.

With all my greed showing I decided to wait just a bit longer to see if prices wouldn't come back. You know the rest. Of course they didn't come back and by the time I sold I had a gain of about $150 per contract whereas the profit, had I sold when I should, would be been about $2,000. All because I failed to act quickly enough.

At times we act too quickly, and at other times, too slowly. What common denominator will tell us when to act correctly?

For one thing, we usually act too quickly when we are trying to make money and too slowly when we are trying to protect our money. When you are pressed to make a decision, ask yourself, "Am I doing this to protect my money or to make more money?" If the answer is to protect money, act more quickly. If the answer revolves around making more money — act slowly.


## THE RAT RACE AND COMMODITY TRADING


At the same time I was busy making my million dollars in the commodity markets, I was also running two other successful businesses.

If I had to do it all over again, I would not divert my attention to anything but the commodity market.


As I've mentioned several times, the market is a cruel lover. It demands all you have. For that reason, it seems the trader should be expending all of his energies on the market. Forget about stocks, real estate, bonds, new issues, etc. You must focus entirely on commodities. Trading is a full-time, 24 hour-per-day job.

By the same token, when you pull out of the market to take a vacation, you should pull out 100% so that your mind can recuperate. When the market gets too hard on you and the pressures too much to bear, leave it alone. Walk away, but do it all the way. Don't leave one or two positions. Make a clean break.

There are several reasons for this advice. First, when people do go on vacation, they fail to leave stops because they think they'll be watching the market on "a pretty close" basis. This is very dangerous. Either vacation, or stay at your desk and work. One fellow I know tried to do both and his $100,000 portfolio slipped to $45,000 in two short weeks. Some vacation that was!

Another reason for telling you to totally clear out of your positions when on vacation is that if you don't do this, your mind will stay in the market rut. You will not be able to refresh your creative cells.

Why even go on vacation if you're going to hold onto positions?


## RANDOM THOUGHTS ON A NON-RANDOM MARKET


Since this appears to be a rather rambling chapter, (and I suppose every book must have one) I'm going to take advantage of it and continue rambling a bit more. I'd like to talk about some non-market things that have been a tremendous help to me in the market.

The first is my own physical conditioning. A few years ago when Bobby Fischer played chess with the Soviet champion (and whipped him soundly) I gained a good deal of insight into the market and intellectual prowess. While the Russian was in training, studying all the moves, Fischer, who totally demolished Spatzky, was also getting ready. But his was physical training. He jogged, swam, lifted weights, watched his diet. To be as powerful as he was, Bobby honed his mind and body to a razor's edge. He spent almost as much time getting into physical shape as mental shape.

That's the way it should be for market traders as well. Without a doubt, my best performances have come when I'm in my best physical condition. Centuries ago, Plato told all of his students to maintain their health and physical condition at optimum levels if they were to be among his best students.

More recently, it's been demonstrated (see Psychology Today) that executives in physical training are more creative, more resourceful and tend to arrive at better decisions more rapidly than their non-athletic counterparts.

I'm not suggesting you become Mohammed Ali. All I'm saying is if you're a bit chunky around the waist, a little flabby in the legs, and get short of breath from lifting your pen (much less a good walk) you'd better pay some attention to your physical well-being. You need every ounce of it for the market.

## STICK TO YOUR GAME PLAN

Later on I'll be telling you about my game plan for market success. In time you'll develop your own, but, like me, you'll go off the plan, meet with problems, and then go back to the plan. It's almost like dieting. It's easy to lose weight when you're on a good diet. So it is with the market. Follow your plan and you'll be quickly separated from your hard earned green. Why even map out a game plan if you're not going to follow it?

The single greatest cause of market loss is the inability to develop or follow a rational program. My greatest weakness, and yours too, will be that of straying from the path you've set for yourself.


## RELAX YOUR WAY TO EASY STREET

I've also found it useful (but oh so difficult) to relax because the daily battle of supply and demand creates a knot in my mind. It is vital that we find the time to relax our mental processes. This can be done through meditation, a hobby, some very physical or demanding activity that forces your mind into the sport and away from the market. For me, fishing and handball fill the bill. For someone else it may be golfing, bowling, collecting stamps or acupuncture.

It matters little how you do it — just as long as you do it.

It is now time to show you the pathway to market success. The doors I'm about to open can change your entire lifestyle. This method works. It will take you a bit of time to catch on but you can do it by carefully reading, contemplating and understanding the following few pages.

CHAPTER TWO

MY KEY INGREDIENT TO MARKET SUCCESS

# CHAPTER TWO

## MY KEY INGREDIENT TO MARKET SUCCESS

### HOW WINNERS END UP LOSERS

Although I manage to make a good deal of money from the commodity market, I am by no means the best forecaster of future prices. Yet, I survive while the real wizards of forecasting fall into bankruptcy. I manage to keep ahead of the game; not so much by outsmarting the other players as by correctly managing my money.

Let me give you an example. One of the many brokers I know likes to specialize in just a few commodities. His favorite is sugar, and his sugar forecasts have, indeed been excellent. I have never taken the time to run a thorough check, but I would say this man's batting record (with the sugar market) is about 80% correct . . . way above the average.

More importantly, Bret (an alias, of course) has been able to see the big moves in sugar and correctly forecast their duration. In spite of this "talent", Bret was wiped out in the sugar market in the spring of 1973! Imagine — a person with almost 20/20 foresight, and he still wound up a loser, on the verge of bankruptcy, humiliated before his firm, friends and clients.

Bret's disaster was precipitated by his lack of money management knowledge. Or, if he did have the knowledge (and I strongly suspect this to be the case) he neglected to pursue the proper path.

His findings suggested that March 1973 sugar would move from the six cents area to the ten cent area thereby creating a gain of $4,000 for each $1,000 invested. Bret began his buying correctly between $5.75 and $6.00. From that level he was delighted to see the market rise immediately to $8.50, thereby doubling his money.

At this particular point Bret sold and waited for a new buying opportunity. For each $10,000 he now had $20,000. When he saw another buying point at $7.50, he re-entered the market using all of the $20,000.

Although prices were to rise later to 10¢ as Bret had forecast, they now dipped and within seven days his new sugar position showed a loss of $10,000 where he was stopped out. Bret was now back where he had started despite the fact that the decline on the bad trade was much less than the rally on the good trade. This came about because he had bought more contracts on the second trade than he had on the first.

9

Bret had moxy . . . and was not to be broken by one bad trade. He was back in the market before long making a valiant effort to prove that he was stronger than the market. He was certainly going to show 'em!

And show them he did. Reinstating his sugar position at $7.50, he gleefully watched it soar to $10.50. He was back on the winning side. His equities were now so large he decided it would be safe to pyramid, or double up his bet. For each contract he bought at $7.50, he now added three more contracts. He was positioned for the big move. Unfortunately, it never came.

In fact, the very next day (and that's the way it usually happens) sugar collapsed. The sweet stuff dropped $1.50 before Bret managed to get out of the market. At this point he was insolvent.

It happened because he had three contracts, long at $10.50, covered at $9.00 (or a loss of $5,040) versus his profit on the position taken at $7.50 which showed a profit of only $1,680 when he finally forced out of the market.

Despite Bret's amazingly correct forecasts, he wound up a loser because he pyramided . . . increasing the size of his position as the market advanced.

In another instance, I personally know of a trader who had $250,000 and saw it diminish to zero within five short weeks. This man's problem was the same as Bret's, only he developed his problem a bit differently. Instead of pyramiding, he plunged — putting his sizeable $250,000 bankroll on higher cattle prices. He went to his market demise when cattle fell out of the barn limiting down and wiping out many investor-traders, including this "big-money" player. The old adage . . . "all the eggs in one basket" is fittingly apropos here.

Plunging is the cardinal sin in money management. Pyramiding will, in most cases, end by establishing you in a position similar to plunging.

## HOW TO MANAGE MONEY AND ELIMINATE MARGIN CALLS

The above disasters are not uncommon. There were worse ones, many of which led to suicides, embezzlements, etc., and would have been totally avoided if the parties had followed my money management philosophy. It is based on the firm conviction that I should never have too many trades at any one given time; never expose myself to too much risk; and never to invest too large a per cent of my capital. Here is my three phase method.

10

## THE 30% STOP RULE

This is the key rule upon which rests the ultimate success in commodity trading. Follow it and you will succeed — win, even when you are losing. Should you show even the slightest disrespect for this rule, I certainly hope you have good connections for a quick loan — you'll need it! The market will wipe you out, right down to the very last penny, and then some, if you fail to heed this advice. I tell you this is an absolute certainty.

My 30% stop rule is simply this. As soon as you have invested 30% of your total funds designated for the commodity market, STOP INVESTING. The same rule applies to the stock market but you can take the per cent up to 50 since stocks are much less volatile.

This means you must first allocate the dollar amount of money with which you wish to trade. The more money you can allocate, the greater your chances for success. Incidentally, let's say life has been good to you and you decide to allocate $20,000 to commodities. I strongly suggest and urge you to take all $20,000 and give it to your friendly broker.

Your next stop is to begin trading (as I'll explain elsewhere). When the cost of your total positions reaches $6,000 you must stop adding new positions. Remember — follow this rule and you will succeed; neglect it, and you will lose.

For a new trader, and for a trader lacking experience, I admonish you to reduce the 30% figure to 20%.

As long as you never commit more than 30% of your funds you can never be totally wiped out. You will make errors — we all do — all the time, but you will still have enough capital and resilliency to bounce back for the next good trade.

There will be times when you will want to press your luck and use 50 to 90 per cent of your equity. Well, that's fine, but don't give me any credit for your gains or your losses. I want no part of that type of speculative activity. I can make all the money I want; 100% a year and more, using 20% to 30% of my total commodity equity. So can you. Don't place yourself in a position that can result in trouble and tragedy.

Rule number two is a very old adage. I imagine its not only one of the oldest on the street but probably the least followed as well. It is, simply, "Use Stops". It means, get out of weak positions, cut your losses short, ad nauseum. It is the one phrase that every book and market letter bandys about but never actually uses!

Trading commodities is an extremely risky venture. It has financial, emotional and physical properties capable of completely wiping out thousands of players in one fell swoop. It has sent thousands to an early demise, split families asunder and been responsible for a host of other devastating experiences. A great deal of this could have been avoided by the use of stops.

By this, I mean one should never have positions in more than six commodities. Once you have seven or more positions you are spreading yourself too thin. You are pushing your luck. I'll use myself as a prime example. I'm supposed to be reasonably bright and rumored to be well educated with the proper degrees, etc. I have also devoted my entire adult life to the market place. I can tell you where Corn sold in July of '34, or what price Winnipeg Flax went off the boards in November of '65. I spend practically my entire working day poring over market statistics, watching, judging . . .

But, for the life of me, I cannot keep track of more than eight positions.

I really don't think you can either. Now don't take that as a challenge. There is no need to prove anything to me or to yourself. This is a simple fact of doing business. Once we take on too many positions, we are going to get lost in the shuffle and lose money. We will either forget to watch what we should be watching, or will have pressed our luck too far in taking on so many positions.

In all my trading I have never been right when I have pressed the market and taken on any large number or size of positions. When we are so damned certain of our success we simply cannot be right in this business. Abide by that, please!

## HOW TO KNOW WHEN YOU ARE OVER-EXTENDED

Just telling you to never carry more than six positions is probably not quite enough. Perhaps I had better embellish on this point. There are times when carrying only two positions can put you under excessive pressure and expose you to an amazing amount of risk.

The surest way to know that you are pressing your luck — that you are just about to take a shelacking — is when you suddenly feel omnipotent! My good friend, Mort Cleveland, says it's when you develop that King Kong feeling and the certain knowledge that Fay Wray is going to hop into bed with you!

Well, I never thought too much about the possibilities of Fay Wray, but I most assuredly do know that feeling. You honestly begin to feel there's no end in sight; that you have the world by the tail and will make your million dollars no later than next Friday. This feeling usually reaches its peak during the first hours of trading on the day you are about to take your bath. When it happens, you have no alternative but to sell all your positions and wait for reason to return. Remember, they got King Kong in the end!

## MY UNIQUE PYRAMID SYSTEM THAT ALMOST GUARANTEES PROFITS

### HOW A SQUARE CAN BE A PYRAMID

My hot-shot trading friends always push their luck to the hilt, constructing all kinds of fancy pyramid plans to make them millions of dollars. They think I'm a bit square. I don't swing money around the way they do. My pyramid plan is to be square. They think I'm too conservative, and maybe I am. But, I think I have the last laugh because they have yet to make any money in the market let alone the million dollars that I've made.

### HOW TO SET STOP POINTS

Just between us, I've always had trouble deciding where to put stops. Bill Meehan, a true commodity genius and to whom I owe a great deal of my success, taught me about stops. Not until then was I able to use them successfully.

Bill's ideas on stops are so brilliant I had to stop thinking about the market for at least a week in order to absorb what he had taught me.

Bill's concept is that stops should be used to protect capital. That is the sole function of stops. Thus, one need not worry about where the stop should be placed with regard to chart or price action. Placing a stop below today's close has nothing at all to do with preservation of capital. The concept Bill originated (along with many other revelations) is that a stop should be your means of preventing under risk. To my way of thinking, this means one should carry a stop on all trades so that if the trade is wrong it will not destroy more than 5% of your total capital. This means; if you have an account of $10,000 you cannot allow any position to lose more than $500.00.

13

If you follow this rule closely, it will take twenty trades in a row on the wrong side of the market before you are out of the game. If you've got a system that "accurate", you should be writing this book, not me!

One hard, iron clad rule is to always set stops that will see you losing no more than 5% of your capital. This is a rule to which you must adhere if you are following in my footsteps.

## HOW TO KNOW THE NUMBER OF CONTRACTS TO BUY

I determine how many contracts of a particular commodity I will purchase by first deciding how much of a decline I'm willing to sit through. A limit and a half is about all I will usually endure.

Let's take cattle as an example. Suppose I am managing $20,000. Naturally, I will be following my 5% loss formula. This means I can lose $1,000 and still have 95% of my equity left.

Should I decide that I don't want to ride the position for more than 100 points, or $400.00, I know I can purchase two contracts and my loss of 100 points, or $400.00, times two contracts, will be $800.00. This is well within my 5% loss rule, telling me that all I can handle is two contracts. I will not take on three.

I arrive at the stop by determining risk exposure — through a combination of chart searching and insight that comes from doing this for many years. As you must know, there are many gray areas to any competitive market. Thus, there are never any absolute answers for exactly how to proceed.

We have no statutes or precedent setting cases to which we can refer. We must hope the great spirits of La Salle Street walk with us from time to time.

This does not prevent us from using common sense which dictates that a 5% loss is the maximum to which we will expose ourselves. In turn, this 5% figure will tell us the number of contracts we can buy or short.

## HOW TO WIN EVEN WHEN YOU ARE LOSING

If you meticulously follow the aforementioned plan for managing money, you will be able to win in the market even when all your positions are in the red. Incredible as it may seem, this is true. By following the above guidelines, you will have eliminated the market's most frequent cause of failure — fear, and inadequate capital.

Yes, by following the plan you will not be plagued with margin calls — there is plenty of margin in your account. You will have your sanity and enough money to bounce right back even under the most adverse conditions.

By contrast, the poor fellow who plunges, does not use stops, and trys to follow seven or more trades, will be beaten to a bloody frazzle by the interworkings of the market. If he doesn't lose his money he will lose the courage to step in for the next good trade.

You can only be prepared for action if you are mentally and financially ready. Maintain that stance at all times. A few words from folk singer, Joan Baez, may help make my point more clear.

> " . . . how many times have you heard some one say,
> 'if I had his money I would do things my way'
> But the world's richest man is a pauper I find
> Compared to the man with a satisfied mind . . ."

Maintain that sense of internal satisfaction and the market becomes much easier. Perhaps it's merely a facade, but that feeling of inner ease and well-being can only be maintained by correctly managing your money.

## PUTTING IT ALL TOGETHER

In this chapter, I have stressed the importance of money management. Hopefully, you will have learned that you must treat your capital in an organized fashion just as any business man. You will not plunge or pyramid. You will know how many contracts to buy, how many positions to have, and how large a loss you will take.

More perceptive readers will more than likely use stops that represent a loss of 2% to 3% rather than the 5% figure I have given. That's fine . . . you can adjust the stop figure in that direction but don't get generous with your money and extend it beyond 5%.

Affix these rules firmly in your mind, and then act by them.

1.  Establish the total dollar amount of your commodity fund.

2.  Give the total amount to your broker. (If your funds exceed $20,000 it would be wise to instruct your broker to buy $10,000 or more of Treasury bills so the money you are holding in reserve — 70% of your capital — is earning interest.)

3.  Stop investing when you have used 30% of the equity in your capital. Do not take on any new positions.

4.  Never allow a position to lose more than 5% of your capital.

5.  Never carry more than six positions at one time. You will be more successful with three to four positions. Don't spread yourself too thin.

6.  Do not pyramid or plunge . . . ever!

7.  Determine how many contracts to buy and do not exceed this limitation.

8.  Use stops based on a % of loss.

CHAPTER THREE

MY FRANK ADVICE FOR BEGINNERS

## CHAPTER THREE

## MY FRANK ADVICE FOR BEGINNERS

### THE IMPORTANT DIFFERENCE BETWEEN STOCKS AND COMMODITIES

Virtually every commodity trader I've met was initially baptized in the fires of the stock market. From this humble beginning traders move to the commodity market because 1 — they realize that's where the action is, or, 2 — they no longer have enough money to maintain a stock account.

Since most people enter the stock market first and then graduate to futures, they have little understanding of commodities. Additionally, the mass media have sorely neglected the commodity markets. While we are given the hourly DJIA changes on most radio stations and nightly market re-caps on major TV networks, they don't give a run-down on the workings of America's fastest moving market.

The beginner in commodities is further stymied because most brokers are not licensed to handle commodities. All investment counselors are gun shy of commodities and financial writers seem to have a passion for scaring the neophyte out of this potentially rewarding area. Perhaps they're right, but my bank account doesn't seem to substantiate that reticence.

Commodities bear little resemblance to stocks. About the only thing they have in common is they are traded in a free bidding market. At that point, all resemblance ends.

Stocks represent what may happen to a company, or at best, the price of the company's shares. No one in the world needs to buy 100 shares. There are no true intrinsic needs for certificates.

Obviously, this is not true of commodities. They are "for real." People must eat Corn, Eastman Kodak must utilize Silver. At times, farmers produce too many Soy Beans and surpluses build. At all times the future price of a commodity is based on the reality of supply and demand. With a stock, there is absolutely no true supply/demand because no one must own a single share of any stock. There is no strong motivating factor as with commodities.

The future price of a stock is based largely upon the myth that earnings will get better, or worse, and earnings alone may not always create a price increase. With commodities, prices are directly related to true supply/demand elements.

Because of this fact, commodity markets are more honest and certainly easier to forecast. I say this because we can determine which factors are controlling the market; largely the commercial interests that must buy commodities. General Mills would be a prime example. They must buy or sell Wheat and, as a rule, these commercial groups are pretty good at what they do. It all boils down to separating the smart players from the not-so-smart, thus arriving at a pretty fair picture of future prices.

The commodity trader has another good advantage — and this is selection.

I know nothing about the market except that I want to learn and want to open an account with him. I would ask for a quick course in the basics, i.e., margins, the

worth of a move, etc. This information will not enable you to make any money in the market. In fact, I would stay away from any broker who tries to push you into trading at that point. All you are seeking is an education in the mechanics of the market.

A good brokerage firm will be able to provide you with a listing of the current margin requirements as well as the value of a 1¢ move for the actively traded commodity market. Keep this list so you can determine how much money you will be making. Below is just such a list. However, margins change, so don't rely solely on this list.

| COMMODITY | Exchange & Trading Hours (N.Y. Time) | Contract Unit | Minimum Fluctuation Per lb., bu., carton, etc. | Per Contract | Maximum Fluctuation (C) Daily Limit | Daily Range | CEA Reporting Level |
|---|---|---|---|---|---|---|---|
| Barley | Winnipeg Grain Ex. 10:30 - 2:15 | 5,000 bu. | ⅛¢ | $6.25 | 10¢ | 20¢ | None |
| Boneless Beef | Chicago Mercantile Ex. 10:15 - 1:45 | 36,000 lbs. | .025¢ | $9.00 | 1.50¢ | 3.00¢ | 25 Contracts |
| Boneless Beef, Imported | N.Y. Mercantile Ex. 10:15 - 1:45 | 30,000 lbs. | .02¢ | $6.00 | 1.50¢ | 3.00¢ | 25 Contracts |
| Broilers (Effective April '72) | Chicago Board of Trade 10:15 - 2:05 | 28,000 lbs. | .025¢ | $7.00 | $2.00 | $4.00 | None |
| Cattle | Chicago Mercantile Ex. 10:05 - 1:40 | 40,000 lbs. | .025¢ | $10.00 | 1.00¢ | 2.00¢ | 25 Contracts |
| Cattle, Feeder | Chicago Mercantile Ex. 10:05 - 1:40 | 42,000 lbs. | .025¢ | $10.50 | 1.00¢ | 2.00¢ | 25 Contracts |
| Choice Steers | Chicago Board of Trade 10:10 - 1:50 | 40,000 lbs. | .025¢ | $10.00 | 1.50¢ | 3.00¢ | 25 Contracts |
| Cocoa | N.Y. Cocoa Ex. 10:00 - 3:00 | 30,000 lbs. | .01¢ | $3.00 | 1.00¢ | 2.00¢ | None |
| Coffee (C) | N.Y. Coffee & Sugar Ex. 10:30 - 2:45 | 37,500 lbs. | .01¢ | $3.75 | 2.00¢ | 4.00¢ | None |
| Copper | N.Y. Commodity Ex., Inc 9:45 - 2:10 | 25,000 lbs. | .05¢ | $12.50 | 2.00¢ | 4.00¢ | None |
| Corn | Chicago Board of Trade 10:30 - 2:15 | 5,000 bu. | ⅛¢ | $6.25 | 8¢ | 16¢ | 200,000 bu. |
| Cotton (#2) | N.Y. Cotton Ex. 10:30 - 3:00 | 50,000 lbs. | .01¢ | $5.00 | 2.00¢ | 2.00¢ | 50 Contracts |
| Eggs, Shell (Effective March 72) | Chicago Mercantile Ex. 10:15 - 1:45 | (750 cases) 22,500 doz. | .05¢ | $11.25 | 2.00¢ | 4.00¢ | 25 Contracts |
| Fish Meal | Int'l Commerce Ex. (N.Y. Produce) 9:45 - 2:45 | 100 metric/tons | 5¢ | $5.00 | $5.00 | $10.00 | None |
| Flaxseed (Mpls) | Minneapolis Grain Ex. 10:30 - 2:15 | 1,000 bu. | ⅛¢ | $1.25 | 15¢ | 30¢ | 200,000 bu. |

| | | | | | | | |
|---|---|---|---|---|---|---|---|
| Flaxseed (Wpg) | Winnipeg Grain Ex. 10:30 - 2:15 | 1,000 bu. | ⅛¢ | $1.25 | 15¢ | 30¢ | None |
| Hogs | Chicago Mercantile Ex. 10:20 - 1:50 | 30,000 lbs. | .025¢ | $7.50 | 1.50¢ | 3.00¢ | 25 Contracts |
| Lumber (Effective May '72) | Chicago Mercantile Ex. 10:45 - 2:15 | 100,000 bd. ft. | 10¢ per 1,000 bd. ft | $10.00 | $5.00 per 1,000 bd. ft. | $10.00 | None |
| Mercury | N.Y. Commodity Ex., Inc 9:50 - 2:30 | (760 lbs.) 10 flasks | $1.00 | $10.00 | $50.00 | $100.00 | None |
| Oats (Chgo) | Chicago Board of Trade 10:30 - 2:15 | 5,000 bu. | ⅛¢ | $6.25 | 6¢ | 12¢ | 200,000 bu. |
| Oats (Wpg) | Winnipeg Grain Ex. 10:30 - 2:15 | 5,000 bu. | ⅛¢ | $6.25 | 8¢ | 16¢ | None |
| Orange Juice (FCOJ) | N.Y. Cotton Ex. 10:15 - 2:45 | 15,000 lbs. | .05¢ | $7.50 | 3.00¢ | 3.00¢ | 25 Contracts |
| Palladium | N.Y. Mercantile Ex. 10:20 - 12:55 | 100 ozs. | 5¢ | $5.00 | $4.00 | $8.00 | None |
| Platinum | N.Y. Mercantile Ex. 9:45 - 1:30 | 50 ozs. | 10¢ | $5.00 | $10.00 | $10.00 | None |
| Plywood (Chgo) | Chicago Board of Trade 11:00 - 2:00 | 69,120 sq. ft. | 10¢ per 1,000 sq. ft. | $6.91 | $7.00 | $14.00 | None |
| Plywood (N.Y.) | N.Y. Mercantile Ex. 11:00 - 2:05 | 70,000 sq. ft. | 10¢ per 1,000 sq. ft. | $7.00 | $6.00 | $12.00 | None |
| Pork Bellies | Chicago Mercantile Ex. 10:30 - 2:00 | 36,000 lbs. | .025¢ | $9.00 | 1.50¢ | 3.00¢ | 25 Contracts |
| Potatoes, Idaho | Chicago Mercantile Ex. 10:00 - 1:50 | (50,000 lbs.) 500 cwt. | 1¢ | $5.00 | 35¢ | 70¢ | 25 Contracts |
| Potatoes, Maine | N.Y. Mercantile Ex. 10:00 - 2:00 | (50,000 lbs.) 500 cwt. | 1¢ | $5.00 | 35¢ | 70¢ | 25 Contracts |
| Propane (L.P. Gas) | N.Y. Cotton Ex. 11:00 - 3:30 | 100,000 gals. | .01¢ | $10.00 | .50¢ | .50¢ | None |
| Rapeseed | Winnipeg Grain Ex. 10:30 - 2:15 | 1,000 bu. | ⅛¢ | $1.25 | 15¢ | 30¢ | None |
| Rye (Wpg) | Winnipeg Grain Ex. 10:30 - 2:15 | 5,000 bu. | ⅛¢ | $6.25 | 10¢ | 20¢ | None |
| Silver (Chgo) | Chicago Board of Trade 10:00 - 2:25 | 5,000 oz. | .10¢ | $5.00 | 10.00¢ | 20.00¢ | None |
| Silver (N.Y.) | N.Y. Commodity Ex., Inc 9:30 - 2:15 | 10,000 oz. | .10¢ | $10.00 | 10.00¢ | 10.00¢ | None |
| Silver Coins | N.Y. Mercantile Ex. 9:25 - 2:15 | $10,000 face value; 10 bags | $1.00 per bag | $10.00 | $100.00 per bag | $200.00 | None |
| Sorghum/Milo | Chicago Mercantile Ex. 10:30 - 2:15 | 200,000 lbs. 3,636.5 bu. | .025¢ per cwt. | $5.00 | 15¢ | 30¢ | 25 Contracts |
| Soybean Meal | Chicago Board of Trade 10:30 - 2:15 | 100 tons | 5¢ | $5.00 | $5.00 | $5.00 | 25 Contracts |
| Soybean Oil | Chicago Board of Trade 10:30 - 2:15 | 60,000 lbs. | .01¢ | $6.00 | 1.00¢ | 2.00¢ | 25 Contracts |
| Soybeans | Chicago Board of Trade 10:30 - 2:15 | 5,000 bu. | ⅛¢ | $6.25 | 10¢ | 20¢ | 200,000 bu. |
| Sugar, Domestic (#10) | N.Y. Coffee & Sugar Ex. 10:00 - 2:50 | 112,000 lbs. | .01¢ | $11.20 | .50¢ | 1.00¢ | None |
| Sugar, World (#11) | N.Y. Coffee & Sugar Ex. 10:00 - 3:00 | 112,000 lbs. | .01¢ | $11.20 | .50¢ | 1.00¢ | None |
| Tin | N.Y. Commodity Ex., Inc 10:20 - 1:45 | 11,200 lbs. | .05¢ | $5.60 | 8.00¢ | 16.00¢ | None |
| Tomato Paste | N.Y. Cotton Ex. 10:45 - 3:15 | 26,500 lbs. | .02¢ | $5.30 | 2.00¢ | 2.00¢ | None |
| Wheat (Chgo) | Chicago Board of Trade 10:30 - 2:15 | 5,000 bu. | ⅛¢ | $6.25 | 10¢ | 20¢ | 200,000 bu. |
| Wheat (K.C.) | K.C. Board of Trade 10:30 - 2:15 | 5,000 bu. | ⅛¢ | $6.25 | 10¢ | 20¢ | 200,000 bu. |
| Wheat (Mpls) | Minneapolis Grain Ex. 10:30 - 2:15 | 5,000 bu. | ⅛¢ | $6.25 | 10¢ | 20¢ | 200,000 bu. |
| Wool, Grease | N.Y. Cotton Ex. 10:00 - 2:30 | 6,000 lbs. | .1¢ | $6.00 | 5.0¢ | 5.0¢ | 25 Contracts |
| Wool Tops | N.Y. Cotton Ex. 10:00 - 2:30 | 5,000 lbs. | .1¢ | $5.00 | 5.0¢ | 5.0¢ | 25 Contracts |

## TERMS YOU MUST KNOW

Just to make certain you can talk about commodities, I'm going to briefly re-cap some of the basic terms. Later, I'll explain the significance of the terms. What is important now is that you understand their meaning.

SHORT SALE — This is similar to shorting a stock. You hope prices will decline so you sell the commodity now, hoping to cover later at a lower price, thereby profiting from the decline.

19

**COMMERCIALS** — are the people who move the market. They are the large buyers and suppliers of the country's commodities. A list must include such corporate giants as Eastman Kodak, General Mills, Pillsbury, etc.

**LOCALS** — are people who trade the market on the floor in Chicago. By and large, they are not an astute bunch.

**FLOOR TRADERS** — There are no specialists in the commodity market, just floor traders and floor brokers. Surprisingly, these people, for the most part, are not great intellectuals. The turn-over on the Chicago Board of Trade is about 50% each year. This tells us that most of these people are losers. But, the winners here do win big.

**TAKING DELIVERY** — Don't believe what your broker tells you about taking delivery of a commodity. With the exception of live animals, Eggs and Cocoa, taking delivery means nothing more than shuffling papers around and paying a few extra dollars. It is usually not expensive to take delivery. Brokerage firms are afraid of it, but from one who has done it, and will do it time and time again, believe me, taking delivery is no big thing. It means you own the commodity. It does not mean the commodity will be shipped to your door!

**LAST TRADING DAY** — This is the last day the commodity contract for that month will trade, i.e., after September 21st, the last trading day in Eggs, there will no longer be a September contract for that year's trading.

### A WORD ABOUT THE WALL STREET JOURNAL

The Wall Street Journal is a great publication and I certainly have nothing against it. However, it has not provided the best, or most comprehensive coverage of the commodity market. Its commodity section leaves a great deal to be desired. It does not follow all the commodities and its volume figures are estimated, not actual figures. Take heart, there is a better source.

I am speaking now about the trusty Journal of Commerce. This excellent publication lists virtually all commodities — even the seldom mentioned ones like Milo, Domestic Sugar, Cross Bred Wool, and Wool Grease.

You will also find The Journal of Commerce the number one reference point for Open Interest (about which you learn more later on) and daily volume. The Wall Street Journal does not give its subscribers Open Interest or Volume for many actively traded commodities.

A subscription costing $42.00 per year may be ordered by writing to The Journal of Commerce at 99 Wall Street, New York, New York 10005. In my opinion, the daily market reviews in The Journal are also superior to those of the Wall Street Journal.

It would appear, on occasion, that the Wall Street Journal is used as a training ground for budding financial writers who can write all about the markets, but tell you nothing. If you are trading commodities and do not get The Journal of Commerce, you're like the man trying to tread water wearing lead boots.

## HOW TO SELECT THE BEST BROKER

Now that you are rapidly learning how to make your millions in commodities, it's time to select a broker and a brokerage firm. First, I'd like to focus on selecting a broker. But, there's something you must understand. To this date, I have never met a broker who has been consistently successful.

That's right, never!

Certainly there are a few who are very good, from time to time, but they always wind up losing their customer and their customer's money. They're all losers. Correct me if I'm wrong. I am not implying that brokers are dishonest or that they have less than your best interests at heart. It's just that their job happens to be one of the most difficult and, unfortunately, they receive no training from their firms with regard to forecasting prices. Firms want salesmen to produce commissions. Whether the customer wins or loses seems to be of little consequence to them.

There are no judicial decisions by which to abide, no dead hurts or questionable calls. We either make money or lose it and our account forms tell the entire story. If your broker cannot produce evidence of his past successes, my advice is to forget him. Therefore, my criteria rules out dealing with a brand new commodity broker unless he has factual data ... brokerage firm transactions ... that prove he's a winner.

Please don't be misled — you can use a broker who is a loser in the market, but only if you use him to execute orders. Asking for his opinion, or seeking his counsel will find you barking up the wrong tree.

My type of broker is the fellow who does not "bug" me with phone calls and who realizes that I am adult enought to make my own decisions, when I want to make them. I will then communicate my needs to him. He is aware that his function is to provide me with information, not opinions, and to get the best possible executions. Anything beyond that transcends a good broker-client relationship as far as I'm concerned.

## THE SMART MONEY WAY TO SELECT A BROKERAGE FIRM

The major area of disenchantment in the commodity market is due, quite possibly, to the calibre of the people with whom you will be dealing. The majority of commodity trading firms are little more than cut-throat, shoe-string operators out to get your very last dollar. They have no finesse, no sense of personal decency. I am specifically referring to the firms that deal only in commodities. Of these I can give my stamp of approval to only two. They are Clayton Commodities and Conti Commodities.

I even have some reservations about these firms. However, that's another story to ponder some late evening over a glass of sherry. I would not have an account with Seigel Trading Company, based solely on general principles.

Ideally, the firm's equity should be over $14 million dollars. The firm you choose must be a clearing member of the various exchanges, not just a member. Thus, you are better protected in the event of the firm's insolvency.

I would venture to say your money is safe with firms that deal in both stocks and commodities. Some of the major firms would be Hayden Stone, E.F. Hutton, Reynolds, Merrill Lynch, Dean Witter, etc. However, I would stay only with the major firms and even then, would not give much credence to their advice. It is far better to become your own advisor than to find yourself hanging on the words of a so-called "expert" who cannot document with his own money the magnitude of his personal success.

## MY LIST OF SUPERIOR ADVISORY SERVICES

Advisory services can, to a limited extent, be of service to you. They will do so by making you aware of trades that might otherwise go un-noticed. They will also provide you with additional insight. If you find a successful service you might even trade on their recommendations. However, after reading this book you should be able to call the shots by yourself.

Advisory services are very much like brokers — they run hot and cold. The publishers are usually broken down, former brokers who are true commodity-holics. If they have the courage to keep track of all their trades and report them in an honest and consistent fashion you can trust them. But, few do just that. My favorite service will obviously include the one I publish, "Commodity Timing." I suggest you write these services, mentioning this book, and ask for a free sample copy for inspection.

**COMMODITIES MAGAZINE 1000** Century Plaza, Columbia, Maryland.

Though not an adivsory service, this monthly magazine rates top priority on any list of reading material. Readers are presented with many different technical and fundamental ideas. The graphics are superb. Don't pass this one up.

**COMMODITY RESEARCH BUREAU CHARTS,** One Liberty Plaza, New York, New York 10006

This is mostly a chart service and a very good one at that. The best! Their price is high — about $300 a year — but the weekly service covers all commodities and also includes periodic mailings of weekly and monthly charts. If you rely heavily on charts, this is a "must" service. Those not so "into" charts can find a less expensive service, but none better than this. The Founding Fathers, the Jilers, are to be congratulated.

**COMMODITY CLOSEUP,** Box 2593, Waterloo, Iowa 50703

This little gem is a real sleeper. If you have the time and patience to read and think about Mort Cleveland's comments you will be greatly enlightened. Who else tells you there's no one planting corn 'cause the advisory went out into the fields over the weekend and checked!" Cleveland will also throw a curve at you in the form of commodity price action and various phases of the moon. This is not astrology — this is lunary cycles and we've seen it work often enough to be true believers. This is one of the few services I pay any attention to.

**COMMODITY TIMING,** 850 Munras Ave. #2, Monterey, CA 93940.

Watch Out, This is us — and we're biased. Our biggest problem is that we seem to have very good stretches when everyone gets on the bandwagon. Then we hit the skids for a month or two until we get with it again and make more money. Our net results for 1972, after losses and commissions, was a gain of $24,630. We know of no other service that came even close. If you decide to trade with us make certain you have adequate capital and try to start when we've been in a slump. We always come out of them.

**ACTIVE CYCLES,** Box 5368, Santa Monica, Ca.

Here's a most interesting service. We say this for several reasons; first, because they give you a weekly basis chart for all the active commodities with Open Interest, volume, etc. and ample space for you to keep up the charts. That alone is worth the subscription price. But, you also get a combination of lines or gauges to help you forecast where to buy, sell, and short. The service has been published since 1956 and Alec Stevens, the publisher, has a good feel for the market. You'll want to look at this one.

MADUFF & SONS, 6399 Wilshire Boulevard, Los Angeles, CA
This is a brokerage firm letter. It's not a work of art, but the advice is some of the very best. Read it closely — these guys are good. Ask Fred Colton to send you a sample copy.


THE WORLD OF COMMODITIES, 7701 Forsyth, Suite 300, Clayton, Mo. 63105, published by Clayton Commodities
One of the very best brokerage firm letters. Get on their mailing list right now. But hurry, it's that good.


MARKET VANE, 431 East Green Street, Pasadena, CA 91101
We're not convinced Jim Sibbett is the greatest trader in the world. His letter, however, is highly valuable because it tells what percentage of advisory services are bullish or bearish on a particular commodity. When the majority of advisors are bullish on a commodity (especially if it's in an historic bear trend) you have a beautiful shorting point. Vice versa for buying. The key is to check the historical trend and then buck the collective advice of all the services. Incidentally, that's my adaptation of his service — not his.


SECURITY MARKET RESEARCH CHART SERVICE, Box 14096, Denver, CO 80214
Here is an excellent chart service for $200 per year. Most all commodities are covered and you're also given some oscillator indices for trading the commodities. The oscillator is the difference between a 3 or 4 day moving average and a 10 day average. Or so we suspect. The graphics are great and the charts easy to read. It's another "must" service.

# CHAPTER FOUR


# MY MILLION DOLLAR FUNDAMENTAL SYSTEM

# CHAPTER FOUR

## MY MILLION DOLLAR FUNDAMENTAL SYSTEM

### FUNDAMENTALS: WHY THEY ARE IMPORTANT

As I've mentioned earlier, the commodity market is unique because it is a realistic market based on supply/demand pressures. In turn, these pressures are authentic as they are based upon actual need of commodity processors. Because of this, the overall fundamental structure is of vital importance.

As a trader you must be concerned with the fundamental view. It will dictate whether you are long or short a particular commodity as well as enable you to better evaluate the risk in a position you are taking.

Traders who fail to read this chapter or attempt to disregard fundamentals will certainly find themselves in trouble. More importantly, if you have a good grasp of the fundamentals — where prices should be going — you will meet with greater market success. If you can envision where prices should be going you will be less affected by short term, erratic swings, thus enabling you to hold your positions for maximum gains.

A very successful trader I know has made his killing by sticking to the fundamental tactics I'll show you in a moment, and then holding onto the commodities until he is stopped out (at his original purchase price) or when the fundamental picture changes. This means he's ridden the market to its utmost and has taken gargantuan profits, profits ten times greater than those made by the average trader.

Developing vision is of extreme importance. It enables you to weather the daily storms that bounce prices up and down. It enables you to hold onto your winning positions, creating sizeable profits. The resulting peace of mind is alone well worth the time you'll spend figuring out the fundamental bias.

### TWO DEFINITIONS THAT ARE IMPORTANT

Traditional market devotees have defined fundamentals as revolving around the supply/demand of the commodity. They compare previous years' supply/demand levels while incorporating today's changing production. This is placed into context with prices. The results are the fundamental view.

Another fundamental approach relies on an intrinsic value level. Basically, it implies that a commodity is cheap at a certain point. This is the usual thought pattern we all share toward commodities. Sugar, judging by past standards and current prices, is either cheap or dear.

Without a doubt this is the most dangerous fundamental system to follow. To say that a commodity has an approximate, absolute value, is to deal in an unreal abstract. Pork Bellies, for example, are only worth that which someone will pay for them . . . they may be worth nothing or $5.00 a pound.

The value approach fundamentalists invariably get wiped out in the market because they see something cheap, i.e., down from a previous high level, and begin their buying. At times they are correct but more often than not they are just trying to call the bottom, and that's difficult.

At this point, the value approach player is faced with a dilemma. He knew Bellies were cheap at 50¢ but here they are at 40¢. What does this tell him? Does it tell him he was wrong, or does it tell him to compound his error and buy more? Since Bellies are cheap at 50¢, aren't they really a great buy at 40¢?

The value approach does not allow us to change quickly enough for rapid markets. Stay away from it.

## A SAMPLING OF FUNDAMENTAL TOOLS

You can apprise yourself of standard fundamental statistics with a quick trip to any brokerage firm. The most general approach is to study the government reports. As an example, the USDA releases a report telling of farmers' planting intentions for the coming crop year.

As the crop year develops, additional reports will be issued indicating the approximate size of the crop. Along with the government's reports several brokerage firms are getting into the limelight by issuing reports compiled by polling the various commodity producers. By and large, both reports give the same indications.

On the demand side of the picture you'll be able to obtain reports from the USDA. These are called "Stocks in All Positions" which tells what the farmers are doing with their grains. Are they holding onto it or letting go? These reports attempt to provide an answer.

Additional facets of the demand picture will be observed by noting retail sales, meat sales, the price of pork vs. beef vs. broilers, etc.

An attempt to arrive at a fundamental view of the market based on this approach usually gets me nowhere. I guess I'm simply not sharp enough to put all the facts together.

For this reason I rely on the actions of others to help me determine the fundamental picture. In effect, I evaluate the fundamentals by observing the actions of people whom I have reason to believe can do a better job than myself. Let's discuss this approach.


## MY MILLION DOLLAR TOOLS

My research has uncovered three aspects of the market that tell me what is being done by people smarter than myself. From these three, non-redundant, sources of data I am able to develop a vision of what is in store for the market.


## MY FIRST SMART MONEY TOOL

The simplest data with which to work is the COMMITMENTS OF TRADERS IN COMMODITY FUTURES, released by the USDA about the 10th of each month. This report breaks down the long and short positions held by the large and small traders.

As you might expect, small traders tend to be on the wrong side of the market and larger traders tend to be on the right side of the market. The following Corn chart of 1973, with the monthly ratio of longs to shorts held by large traders, is a good case in point.

As you can see, the large traders anticipated higher Corn prices. Despite a lackluster market in a narrow trading range, the large traders had a sizeable long position particularly when compared to their short position. Followers of these reports had a definite indication to be on the alert for a sizeable move in the Corn market. The handwriting was on the wall for all to see.

Your first fundamental tool will be the large trader report. Please keep in mind that its purpose is to show you where the large traders are and what they're doing. This is not a timing tool. It's function is to alert you to the "deals" you should be scouting out.

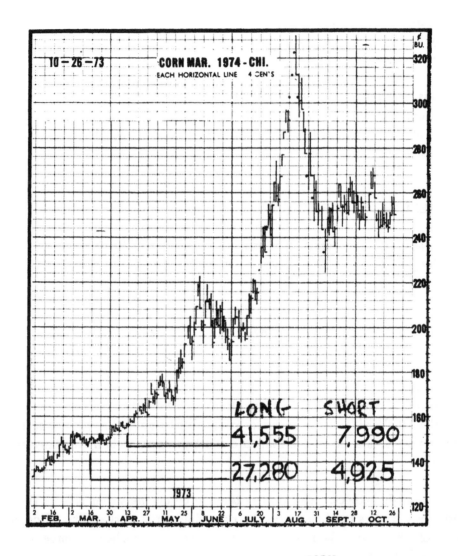

CORN

| LARGE TRADERS | | | (In thousand bushels) | | |
|---|---|---|---|---|---|
| Speculative | | LONG | SHORT | | |
|   Long or short only | | 41,555 | 7,990 | + | 14,275 |
|   Long and short (spreading) | | 44,700 | 42,075 | + | 13,015 |
|   Total | | 86,255 | 50,065 | + | 27,290 |
| Hedging | | 217,588 | 310,740 | − | 34,057 |
| Total reported by large traders | | 303,843 | 360,805 | − | 6,767 |
| SMALL TRADERS | | | | | |
| Speculative and hedging | | 136,147 | 79,185 | + | 24,207 |
| | | | | | |
| TOTAL OPEN INTEREST | | 439,990 | 439,990 | + | 17,440 |
| | | | | | |
| Percent held by: | Large traders | 69.1 | 82.0 | − | 4.4 |
| | Small traders | 30.9 | 18.0 | + | 4.4 |

Commitments of traders, Chicago Board of Trade, April 30, 1973

| Classification | April 30, 1973 | |
|---|---|---|
| | Long | Short |
| LARGE TRADERS          SOYBEANS | (In thousand bushels) | |
| Speculative | | |
|   Long or short only | 18,375 | 20,865 |
|   Long and short (spreading) | 66,315 | 66,195 |
|   Total | 84,690 | 87,060 |
| Hedging | 172,370 | 155,040 |
| Total reported by large traders | 257,060 | 242,100 |
| SMALL TRADERS | | |
| Speculative and hedging | 54,570 | 69,530 |
| TOTAL OPEN INTEREST | 311,630 | 311,630 |
| Percent held by:   Large traders | 82.5 | 77.7 |
|   Small traders | 17.5 | 22.3 |

SOYBEAN OIL

| | Long | Short |
|---|---|---|
| LARGE TRADERS | (In tank cars of | |
| Speculative | | |
|   Long or short only | 8,761 | 10,532 |
|   Long and short (spreading) | 9,113 | 9,113 |
|   Total | 17,874 | 19,645 |
| Hedging | 15,879 | 22,876 |
| Total reported by large traders | 33,753 | 42,521 |
| SMALL TRADERS | | |
| Speculative and hedging | 13,493 | 4,725 |
| TOTAL OPEN INTEREST | 47,246 | 47,246 |
| Percent held by:   Large traders | 71.4 | 90.0 |
|   Small traders | 28.6 | 10.0 |

SOYBEAN MEAL

| | Long | Short |
|---|---|---|
| LARGE TRADERS | (In hundred tons) | |
| Speculative | | |
|   Long or short only | 5,080 | 5,090 |
|   Long and short (spreading) | 3,448 | 3,448 |
|   Total | 8,528 | 8,538 |
| Hedging | 14,205 | 14,441 |
| Total reported by large traders | 22,733 | 22,979 |
| SMALL TRADERS | | |
| Speculative and hedging | 4,329 | 4,083 |
| TOTAL OPEN INTEREST | 27,062 | 27,062 |
| Percent held by:   Large traders | 84.0 | 84.9 |
|   Small traders | 16.0 | 15.1 |

## MY SECOND SMART MONEY TOOL

Your next source of fundamental information will come directly from The Journal of Commerce or the Wall Street Journal. This is one of the most important sources for fundamental data but is passed up by 98% of the players in this game. Let me first explain some workings of the market so you can better grasp the significance of the data.

Typically, a commodity that is going to be delivered in December of this year will sell for more than a commodity that is to be delivered in June of the same year.

That's because the person who must hold onto the commodity until delivery in December will be faced with more holding costs. After all, he will have to pay storage, insurance, and perhaps interest for the months of July, August, September, October, November and December. The person taking delivery in June does not have to absorb these costs.

Therefore, the more distant months of a commodity sell for more than the nearby months.

Write that on a slip of paper and carry it in your wallet. Paste it on your ceiling or stick it to your forehead, but whatever you do, don't forget that lesson. It is the basis for my million dollar fundamental system.

The typical price structure is to see distant months selling at a premium. That is, June 1975 Wheat selling for less than December 1975 Wheat; or July Pork Bellies selling for less than the following year's February Bellies.

A reversal of this price spread is highly signficant as you can perhaps imagine. Such a reversal — when the nearby contracts sell for more than the distant contracts — is concrete proof someone is willing to pay a premium for the product. Someone, someplace wants the commodity so badly that he's willing to pay an extra amount to acquire control of that commodity.

Now, who could it be? Well, when you consider that large traders and the commercials have more money than the public, and commercials are the only ones who really need the commodity, I think you have to conclude the driving force behind such a premium spread is smart money.

In fact, you'll find that all bull markets of any significance are signaled well in advance by the special premium situation I have just pointed out. Ted Rice, while with Continental Grain, one of the world's largest Commodity dealers, is one of the few insiders to tell the public about the importance of this premium spread.

The words from this vice president of this major commercial dealer are fascinating. He has publicly stated that, "we can say carrying charges exist when grain isn't wanted at existing prices."

There it is, words from the real smart money in this game. A carrying charge market, one where distant contracts sell for more than nearbys, means the commodity is simply not in tight demand. The reverse, as you can see, says the commodity is in tight demand and a bull move is on, or about to develop.

Lesson number two in fundamentals is to closely follow the premiums. In a later chapter I'll explain more about premiums. For now, just remember, it is vitally important to follow premium spreads so you can forecast which markets are bullish and which are bearish.


## MY THIRD SMART MONEY TOOL


The third and final million dollar fundamental tool was given to me by Bill Meehan whom I've mentioned earlier. Bill's tactic is to determine what the commercial interests are doing in the commodity market. To fully understand the data you need some of the rationale behind it. Here goes!

To begin with, you should know that the largest short seller in any market tends to be the commercial interests — these are smart money people. This is because the commercials are always in the market spreading and hedging their actual positions.

Certainly, speculators are also short sellers, but the majority of short selling is done by the commercial interests. Knowing this is important because it is possible to keep track of how much short selling is taking place in the market through the use of Open Interest.

Open Interest is the total position of the longs and the shorts in the market. There is a buyer for every seller; in other words, they are evenly matched. The Open Interest figure represents the number of open long and short positions. The figure is available each day on the broad tape as well as in the following day's newspaper.

The Open Interest figures will decline if, and only if, short sellers are covering their shorts. It will rise if, and only if, short sellers are increasing their shorts. Since we know that smart money is responsible for most of the short selling, we can correctly say that an increase in Open Interest indicates an attitude of bearishness of the part of the commercials. A decrease indicates an attitude of bullishness on the part of the commercials.

By itself, the Open Interest figures offer little forecasting value. It is when we team them together with price action that some truly remarkable patterns develop, forecasting some fantastic market moves.

The patterns for which I look are those of price consolidation or trading ranges. When such price action develops, and Open Interest declines during this price action, we are being told commercials feel prices will break out of the consolidation on the upside. We should be buyers.

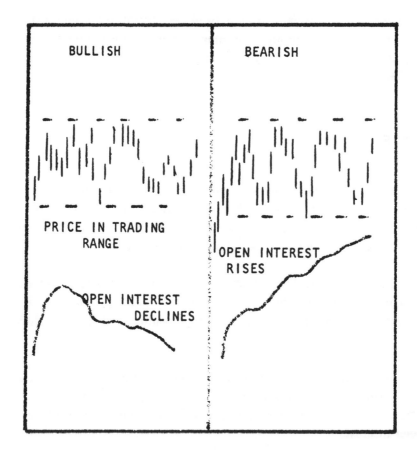

By the same token, a price consolidation or trading period during which Open Interest increases tells us commercials are shorting, looking for prices to break out of the consolidation on the down side.

Ideally, the consolidation pattern will be part of a large up or down move as depicted by the prime example below. This is not always so, but when it is, the odds are all the more on your side.

Notice the example of Open Interest while Copper made a major bottom in 1973. Prices see-sawed back and forth in a trading range while the open interest took a dramatic plunge telling us the commercials were ready for a big bull market. Indeed they were! (Chart not shown.)

32

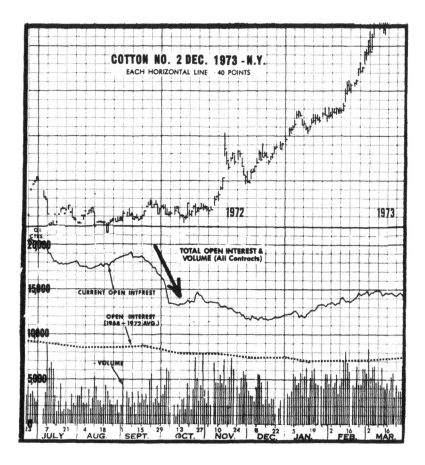

Next, turn your attention to the gargantuan bull move in Cotton — the market that saw Cotton go to its highest price in world history. All this was previewed by a tremendous decline in open interest during the preparatory bottom range.

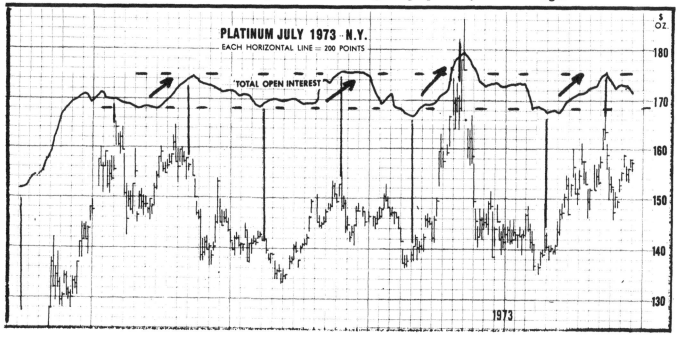

33

Platinum shows a good picture of how Open Interest can help spot tops and bottoms. Notice, as the Open Interest expands to a high level, prices stall and decline until Open Interest falls to a low level from which a rally is given birth. Amazing, isn't it?

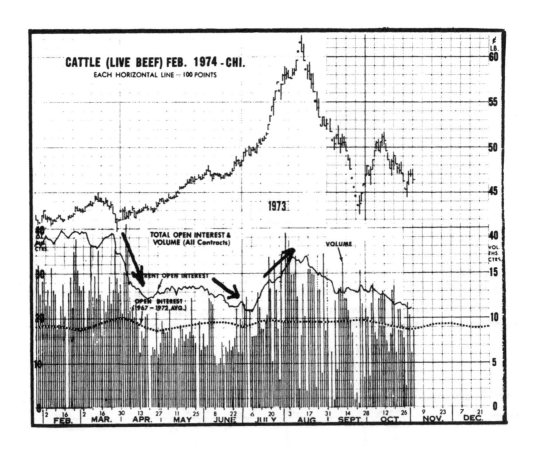

A tremendous slide in the price of Cattle was also forecast by the rapid increase in Open Interest during August 1973. I am also showing unmarked examples of price and Open Interest so you can learn to look for yourself at this interesting relationship. Study it well, it is the third fundamental tool that will help you on your way to a million shiny cartwheels.

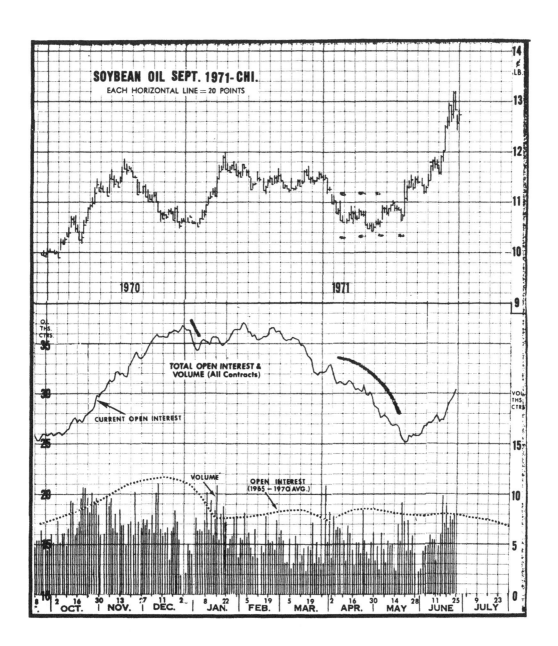

SOYBEAN OIL SEPT. 1971- CHI.
EACH HORIZONTAL LINE = 20 POINTS

1970

1971

TOTAL OPEN INTEREST &
VOLUME (All Contracts)

CURRENT OPEN INTEREST

VOLUME

OPEN INTEREST
(1965 – 1970 AVG.)

OCT. | NOV. | DEC. | JAN. | FEB. | MAR. | APR. | MAY | JUNE | JULY

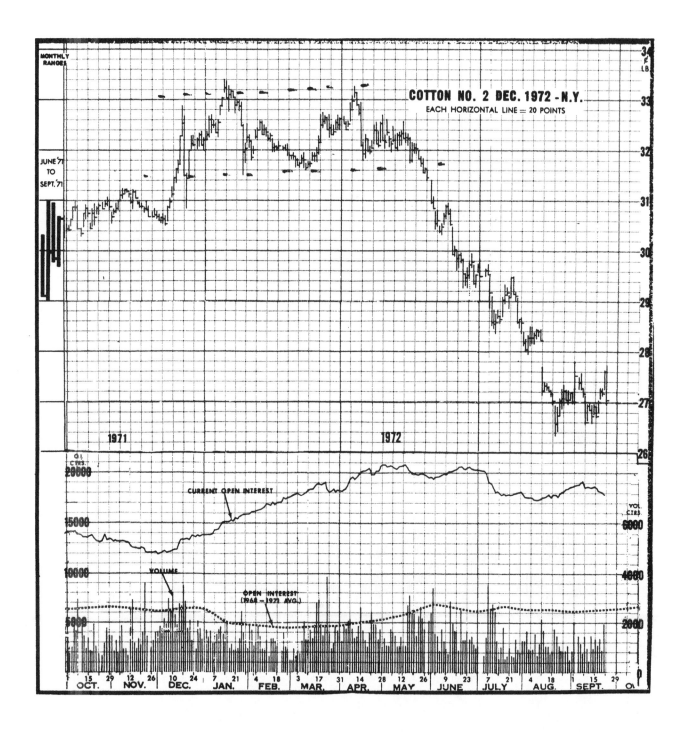

Open Interest used in this fashion is the most valuable market tool I possess. It is the back bone to my success.

36

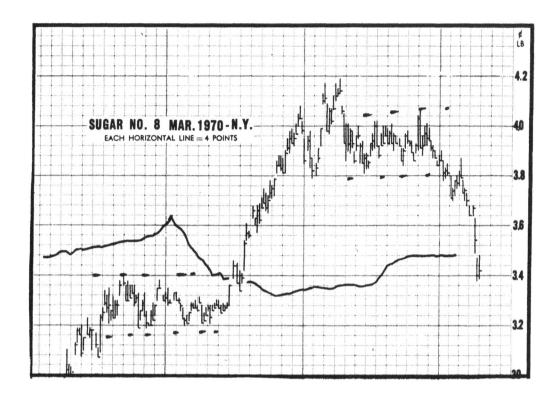

**SUGAR NO. 8 MAR. 1970 - N.Y.**
EACH HORIZONTAL LINE = 4 POINTS

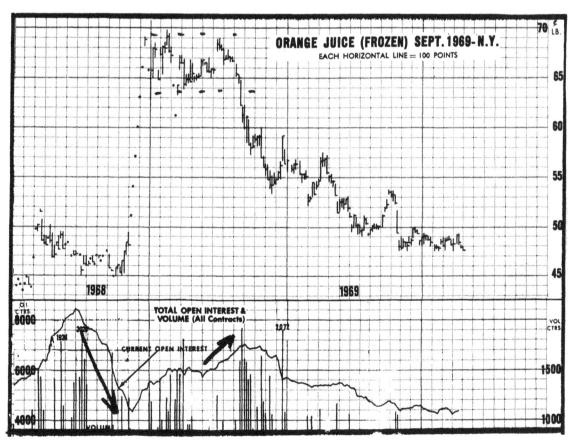

**ORANGE JUICE (FROZEN) SEPT. 1969 - N.Y.**
EACH HORIZONTAL LINE = 100 POINTS

1968

1969

TOTAL OPEN INTEREST &
VOLUME (All Contracts)

CURRENT OPEN INTEREST

VOLUME

## HOW TO EVALUATE ALL FUNDAMENTAL NEWS

One of the biggest problems facing the average trader is the news with which he is bombarded each and every trading day. Russia is buying Wheat. China is selling and the Peruvian fishing fleet just went out while the Oranges are freezing in Florida! What can one do? Is it possible to develop a reasonable method with which to interpret this ever changing and frequently erroneous data?

I think so.

The method I use to judge news is to assume that any story I hear is just that — a story. While I want to hear all the news I have a resolute attitude that news itself means nothing to me.

What does count is the way the market should react to the news and the manner in which the market actually does react. This is really a rather simple strategy. It takes precious little savvy to comprehend the fact that Wheat prices should rally since Rhodesia is buying Wheat. Should the hot lines flash that Brazil has an overproduction of Sugar, even the simplest trader will expect sugar prices to undergo some selling pressures. That would be normal.

In the commodity market it is the deviation from normal patterns that is significant. That's the way to play the fundamental news stories. Should bearish news hit the market, and prices merely shrug it off, you know the market is indeed strong and ready to rally.

Last year the Cattle market showed how valuable this tactic can be. A government report came out; very bullish on the entire complex. The opening indications were that Cattle would be "up the limit". Frankly, I didn't care what was supposed to happen — it was what would happen that was important.

In this case, Cattle futures opened up only slightly telling us the news wasn't really bullish and Cattle prices were weak. Indeed they were. They plummeted 6¢ over the next few trading sessions!

Don't judge the news. Learn to judge the market's reaction to the news and you will be able to master any fundamental news stories.

In closing this chapter I would like to tell you about a hot news story I once received on Bean Oil and Bean Meal. The Peruvian boats had been fishing and bringing in good catches which caused some weakness in the Bean Oil complex. Then came an announcement that the ships had stopped fishing and returned to port. Zingo! Bean Oil went up the limit.

# CHAPTER FIVE

## HOW TO FIND TRADES WITH 10/1 ODDS

The news story continued, saying, "trawlers had returned to port because the catch was so large, the fish so plentiful, that canneries could not keep up with the supply of fish.

Zingo! Bean Oil went down the limit.

All this within a matter of thirty minutes. The person who looked at the news to trade was in trouble either way you look at it. Again, and I repeat myself, follow the impact of the news on the market — not the news itself.

## WHAT TO DO ONCE YOU HAVE MADE YOUR FUNDAMENTAL DECISION

Hopefully, the ideas expressed above will enable you to arrive at the correct fundamental picture. Naturally, it won't always work nor will it answer all questions. But, by and large, it will enable you to be heads and shoulders — in fact, light years ahead of the competition.

Carefully study the large traders for smart money interests. Then, check the premiums to learn what markets are in the tightest demand and finally, seek out trades where the commercials are heavy short sellers or are rapidly covering their shorts.

When you have finally formulated the markets you wish to work, on the bull or bear side, it is time to turn to the technical studies in order to properly time the entry of your purchases and sales. Fundamentals are of little value in timing your entry point but they are important because they dictate your decision to work a commodity from either the short or long side of the market.

What's more, once you are confident of a bull trend you can carry wider stops or take larger positions. You'll also sleep a damn sight better knowing that you are in tune with the true professionals in this business.

It will be important for you to re-evaluate the fundamental appraisal on a month-to-month basis to make certain something has not slipped by your notice. Should conditions change, (and that can happen) be ready to switch from going long to short or vice versa.

You are now fundamentally ready to tackle the world's most challenging markets. It's time to teach you the technical aspects of this business as well as to refine your understanding of the premium spread.

# CHAPTER FIVE

## HOW TO FIND TRADES WITH 10/1 ODDS

Any silly fool can buy and sell commodities whenever he chooses. It is the brilliant trader's task to wait until odds are 10 to 1 in his favor before making a commitment to the market. By doing this the astute trader avoids an immense number of headaches and even greater frustrations.

Obviously, a trader who follows a money management system such as the one I discussed earlier realizes the importance of fereting out the very best possible trades. After all, trading commodities is difficult. Why take any more chances than you have to? Stick with the very best trades and you are bound to come out a big winner.

Whenever I think about the thousands of trades made each day as well as the public's fervor for day trading and short term, (4-5 day trades) I'm reminded of the words from one of the oldest "pros" on Wall Street. This gentleman (you'd recognize his name in an instant) told me that in his forty years of market experience he knew only one commodity winner. Only one!

According to this man, the reason that person was a winner was that he had enough sense to put most of his profits in an irrevocable trust. Thus, when he started to lose, he still had a fixed income from the trusts. Had the trust not been in effect, this "pro" would have lost all that money as well!

Let this be a lesson to you. Don't be eager to rush into any trades. After all, "fools rush in where wise men fear to trade". Hopefully, in this chapter, I can show you how to select the very best possible trades. It's up to you to maintain the discipline required for working the lead-pipe-cinch deals. Discipline, I cannot give you.

## SPOTTING THE BEST TRADES

Let me begin by telling you of my system for isolating trades with odds 10 to 1 in my favor. Those are million dollar odds. Unfortunately, I still haven't developed a method for calling all the big moves all the time. What I have done is develop a set of criteria that will, when they coincide, tell you the odds are heavily in favor of either an up or down move.

This method seldom speaks, but when it does, you have as close to a sure thing as you'll ever get. As you will see, this method will not call all the swings, but that's not its purpose. Its function is to segregate the super trades from trades that are questionable.

Trading in this manner is much easier because it allows you to take a longer term view of the market. I have found there is no need to monitor the market on a trade-by-trade basis, or, at times, even a daily basis. The signals are so strong that you don't need to concern yourself with a microscopic view.

I use two major tools for selecting "bankable trades". They are: 1) premium relationships, and 2) open interest. When these two click, the odds are 75% in your favor. To further substantiate the 75% probability, I also check contrary opinion, the market's reaction to news, trend direction, and a few chart formations.

## THE FIRST INDICATION OF A MILLION DOLLAR TRADE

As you recall, I previously discussed the significance of premiums. I cannot stress this factor too strongly. The existence, or lack of premium will be one of your first keys to a sure thing trade. Premiums, (the difference between the nearby price of a commodity and the distant contracts) give signals in two ways.

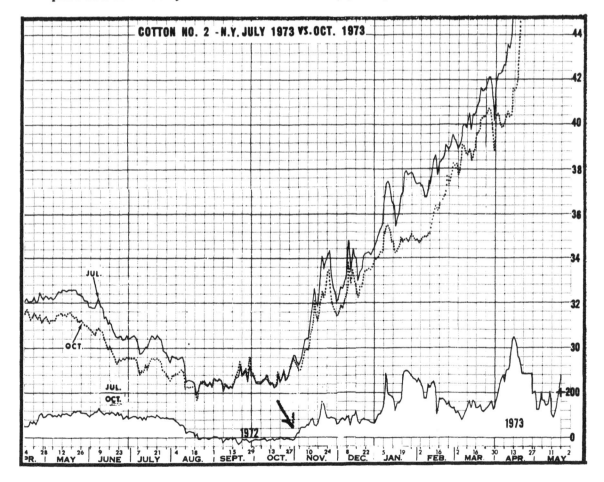

41

The usual bull market signal is given when the nearby contracts sell for a higher price than the distants. Such a spread, in favor of the nearbys, is a bullish premium indicating the commercials want the product now and are willing to bid the market to a "premium". See cotton chart on page 41.

Invariably, sustainable bull markets start with prices going to a premium. If you are looking to go long a commodity, this will be your first check point. Is there a bullish premium? If not, the odds of a sharp advance are not good.

Please notice in the charts, the spread between November and January Orange Juice and the July-October Cotton spread.

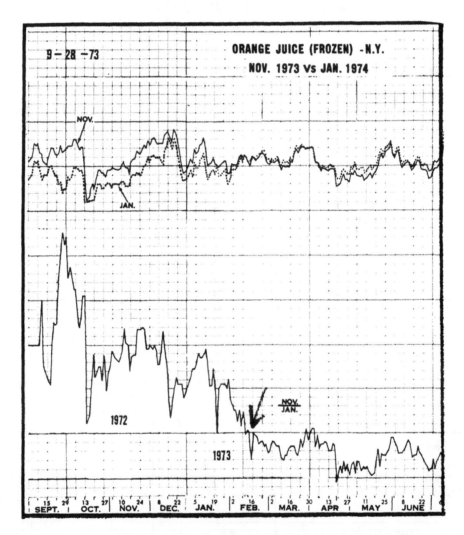

As you can see, the Orange Juice spread went from a premium to a discount. That is, the nearbys sold for less than the distants starting in February 1973. About this same time, many analysts forecast a bull market for Orange Juice, but, as you can see, it could not sustain any up trend. While commodities in general had the largest bull market in history, Orange Juice stayed flat to down.

This was a superb example of the lack of a premium signal telling the trader it's too early to start thinking about higher juice prices.

How about Cotton? This is an entirely different matter. Notice how prices went to a premium in November 1972 while prices were still low. In fact, most services thought this was a major bear market.

We knew better. If Cotton was in a bear market, why would the commercials be willing to pay a premium price for the nearby products. Why not wait until prices went lower in the future? Shortly after this premium developed, Cotton staged the largest bull market it has ever known. Had you bought one contract of December 1973 Cotton the day the premium developed (for $1,000) your profit would have soared to $27,500 in less than 12 months!

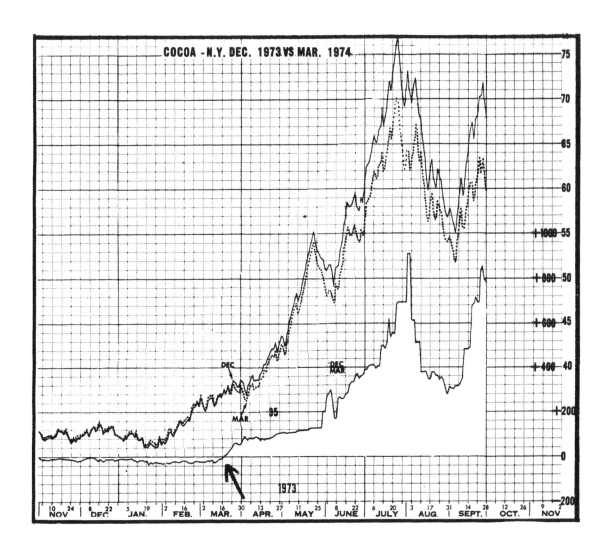

Still doubt the significance of the premium spread? Then study the Coca spread chart paying close attention to the March 1973 time period. This is when a premium developed in the Cocoa market. Sharp shooters will scoff at this method saying it did not call the absolute low in Cocoa. And, they're right. It didn't. But, it did give a strong signal in March telling us that a substantial and sustainable bull move was under way, and that's what we are looking for.

I'll let someone else call the tops and bottoms. What I want is to trade in sure deals. To my knowledge there is absolutely nothing that calls all the tops and bottoms.

In the Cocoa "deal", prices began moving up three weeks after the premium developed giving the trader ample time to prepare for the move. Incidentally, in the case of March 1973 Cocoa, had a trader purchased it when the premium developed in March 1973, (at 37¢) he could have sold it for 71¢, a profit of $10,200 a few months later!

Imagine, the person who bought ten contracts (for $10,000) would have made over $100,000 in less than eight months.

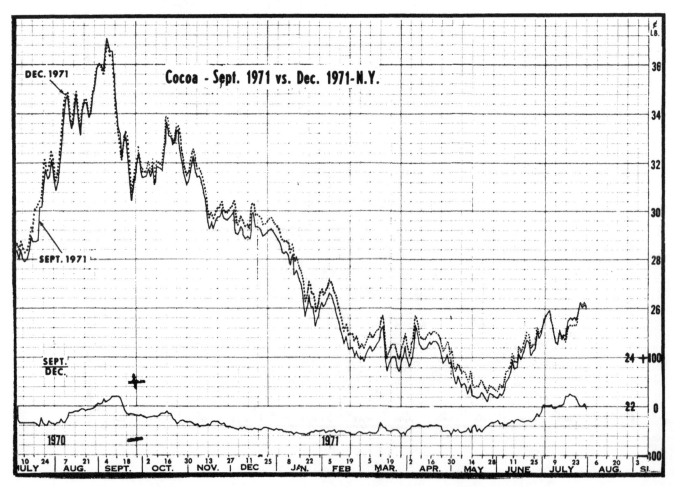

44

Before you mortgage your home and rush out to start buying the premium markets, let me give a word of caution. You still need to know more about the markets to avoid getting tripped up.

Premiums point the way, but they are not an absolute tool nor are they a timing tool. Finally, I ask you to remember that not all bull markets will exhibit premiums. We have other tools with which to isolate the strong, non-premium bull markets. The 1971 bearish Cocoa market was also called quite well by the spread, as you can see.

## YOUR SECOND LESSON ON PREMIUMS

There are many ways to analyze premiums. Rather than confuse you with the various methods I use (I follow the spread in several different fashions) I think it will be best to show you the second most valuable way of using premium spreads.

As the spread between the nearby month and the distant goes to a premium, you have your first indication of a bull market. Now, as this spread increases or decreases we are given additional market information. Essentially, as a premium spread narrows, the market will undergo selling pressures. A rally should start after it begins to widen.

Perhaps this is an overstatement. Let's see.

In September 1971, the Wheat market went into a tailspin. However, the bullish premium was maintained. Then, at the end of September and early October, the spread between May and July started to gain, telling us that the nearby was under commercial buying and a rally should develop. See what happened. A 15¢ rally began which, in those days, was a pretty nice swing!

The 1973 Cotton market also gives us a good indication of the powerful premium signal. Notice the sell-off that started at the end of March. Prices broke sharply, then rallied back to the old highs. What would happen? Was it all over?

Anyone looking at the spread would have seen a sudden increase in the premium of July over October telling us it was still a tight bull market and higher prices were in order. Away went Cotton.

Please don't get the impression I'm a perpetual bull just because I've discussed little else but bull signals to this point. Most commodity traders were wiped out in August of 1973 as the red hot bull market went sour. Traders caught long in that market suffered severe financial and emotional set backs.

45

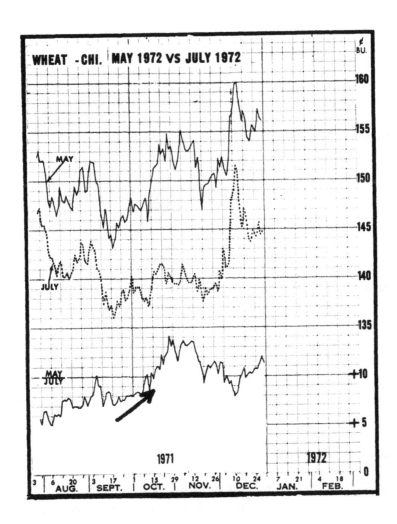

This would not have happened had they been following market premiums. Soy Beans are a good example. Notice how the Bean spread began narrowing as prices were in their final upthrust stages, telling us weakness was due ... that commercials no longer wanted the nearby product.

Now turn your attention to the Cattle market. The same thing occurred. As these important tops were made the premiums fell apart giving ample warning of weakness ahead. That's when it was time to fasten seatbelts. I have shown additional examples for your own study, which is what it takes to understand the premium play.

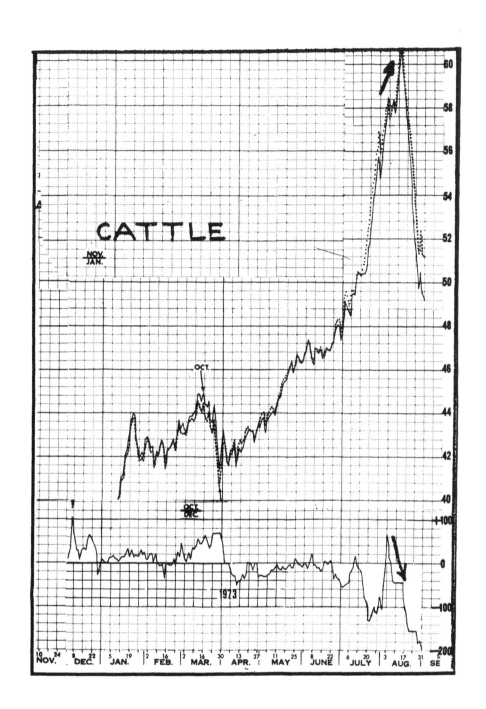

CATTLE

1973

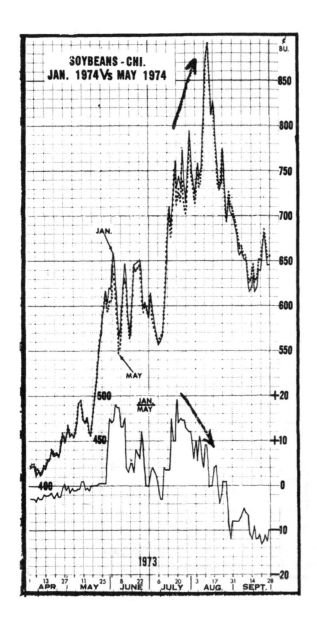

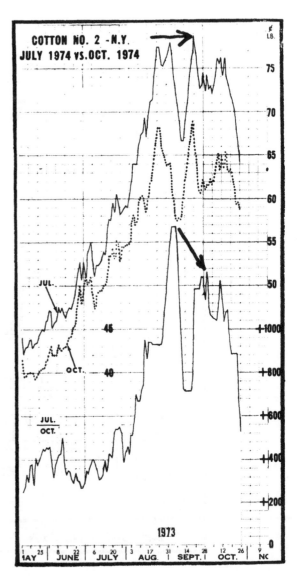

48

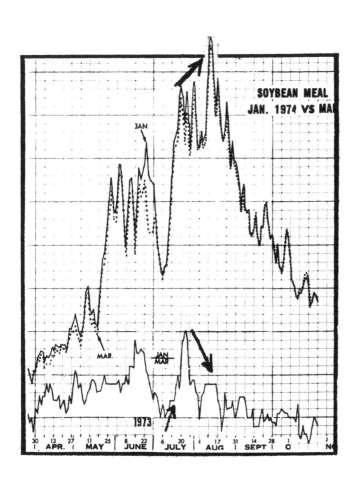

SOYBEAN MEAL
JAN. 1974 VS MA[R]

JAN

MAR.

JAN
MAR

1973

30 | 13 | 27 | 11 | 25 | 8 | 22 | 6 | 20 | 3 | 17 | 31 | 14 | 28 | 1 | O | N
APR. | MAY | JUNE | JULY | AUG | SEPT | O

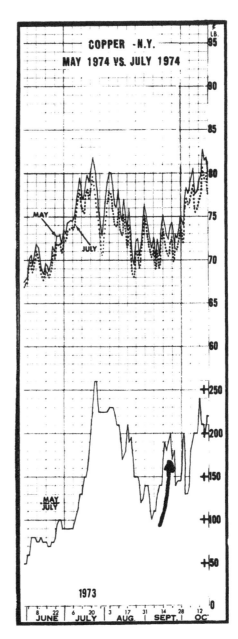

COPPER -N.Y.
MAY 1974 VS. JULY 1974

LB.
85

80

85

80

MAY

JULY

75

70

65

60

+250

+200

+150

+100

MAY
JULY

+50

1973

0

8 | 22 | 6 | 20 | 3 | 17 | 31 | 14 | 28 | 12
JUNE | JULY | AUG. | SEPT. | OC

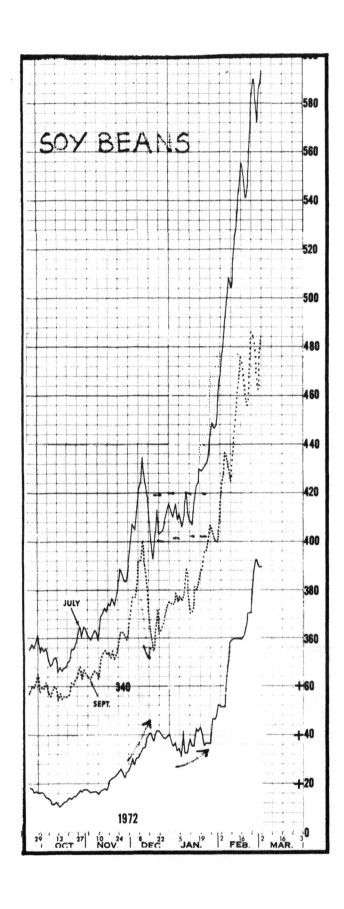

SOY BEANS

Silver - Mar. 1970 vs. Sept. 1970 - N.Y.

SEPT. 1970

MAR. 1970

MAR.
SEPT.

1969

1970

¢
OZ.

220

210

200

190

180

170

0

-5

-10

-15

| 2 | 16 | 30 | 13 | 27 | 11 | 25 | 8 | 22 | 5 | 19 | 3 | 17 | 31 | 14 | 28 | 12 | 26 | 9 | 23 | 6 | 20 |
| MAY | | JUNE | | JULY | | AUG. | | SEPT. | | OCT. | | NOV. | | DEC. | | JAN. | | FEB. | |

10005

51

## THE SECOND INDICATION OF A MILLION DOLLAR TRADE

Earlier I explained Open Interest to you, what it is and how it works. It is important to keep in mind that Open Interest is an accurate reflection of commercial doings. After all, they are the single largest factor in the market. Equally important is the fact the commercials tend to be the largest short sellers because they are hedging their risks. When commercials are not selling short, or hedging, it is because they believe prices are going higher — much higher.

What we look for here is an indication of a lack of short selling among the market's largest professionals. When such a condition develops, especially in a premium market, you have a bankable trade with odds 10 to 1 in your favor.

By the same token, a market without a premium that suddenly sees a large increase in professional short selling, gives you 10 to 1 odds for selling short.

It is my belief that daily Open Interest statistics will correctly tell you if the commercials are selling or covering short positions. The significance of Open Interest cannot be overestimated. Time after time I have made substantial money, and by that, I mean $30,000 to $100,000 per day, thanks to closely following the Open Interest picture.

Open Interest is one of the most widely followed tools. Thankfully, however, it is the most incorrectly interpreted tool. It is the backbone to my success in the commodity market.

Before showing the actual buy and sell signals from Open Interest, I'd like to review Open Interest with you. As you know, it is the total commitment of longs and shorts in the market. Since there is a long for every short, the Open Interest figure is the combination of longs and shorts, divided by two. Only one thing can make Open Interest go up, and that's an increase in short selling and an increase in buying. Only one thing can make Open Interest decline. That's a decrease in buying and a decrease in short selling.

Since the commercials are the dominant force in the market, especially in short selling, an increase in Open Interest would most likely mean they are shorting the market.

A decrease in Open Interest would probably tell us the commercials are covering their short positions, expecting higher prices.

Those two observations have made hundreds of thousands of dollars for me. If there is one page in this book to which you must pay close attention, this is it. Godot has arrived!

The inset shows the basic buy and sell indications given from the Open Interest figures. It is imperative that you understand the relationship of price vs the Open Interest. As you can see (inset)/the bullish pattern shows prices in a trading range while Open Interest is decreasing. Hence, the commercials have covered their shorts.

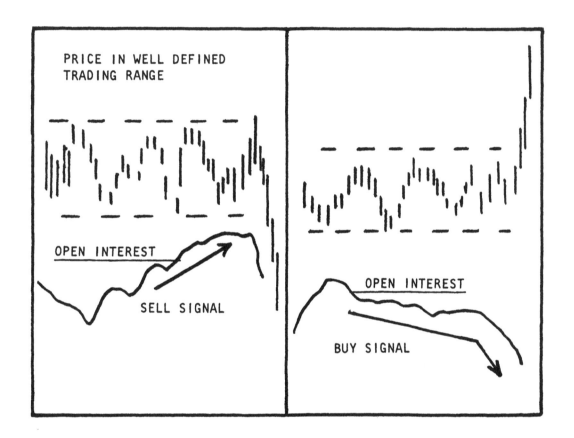

The bearish pattern also sees prices in a trading range while Open Interest increases. Ideally, for short selling, the trading range will be part of a large down move or will occur at a time when the nearby contracts are strong and the more distant months weak. This sets up a "sure" trade.

If you were to close the book at this point and begin using Open Interest you could probably smoke out some pretty fair trades. However, you might also fall into some extraordinarily bad deals. I have not yet fully emphasized the importance of the trading range.

A simple increase or decrease in Open Interest — without prices being in a trading range — is of little significance. You must compare the Open Interest picture with the price action. In a moment, I'll give you some actual examples.

The few people to whom I have shown the Open Interest signals have been amazed at its accuracy in selecting long term trades. However, they always try to apply Open Interest to all commodities, all the time. It just doesn't work that way. After all, we are trying to select the cream of the crop trades where there is little, if any risk. We are not attempting to call every market wiggle and waggle. This means we must adhere to our game plan and that plan calls for finding optimum trades.

There is one other Open Interest pattern for which you should be alert. This occurs amidst a major bull or bear market. In a major bull market, i.e., strong uptrend, prices will suddenly react against the maintrend; falling sharply. If, at this time, open interest diminishes, a buy point is being set up.

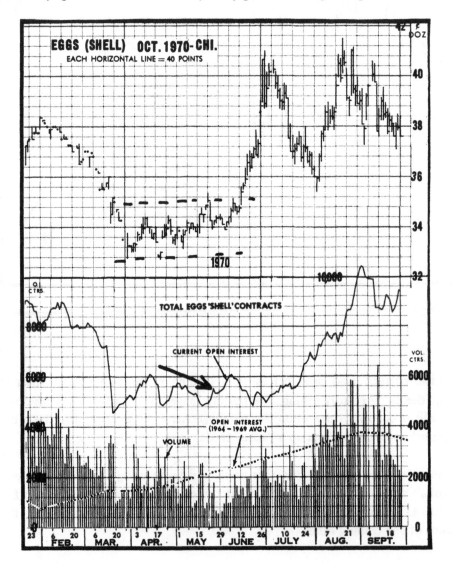

54

In a strong bear market, a rally against the trend (accompanied by an increase —
especially a large increase in Open Interest) is very bearish, setting up a shorting
point.

Incidentally, when I talk about increase in Open Interest, I should point out that
a 25% increase or decrease is enough to greatly excite me. Anything less than 25%
may be due to the market's idiocyncrasies rather than commercial action.

If you'll take the time to study any chart service that plots Open Interest you'll
quickly see major buy and sell indications. As an example, in April and May of
1970, Open Interest declined while the price of eggs stayed in a tight trading
range thereby foretelling higher prices. As you can see, this is exactly what did
ensue.

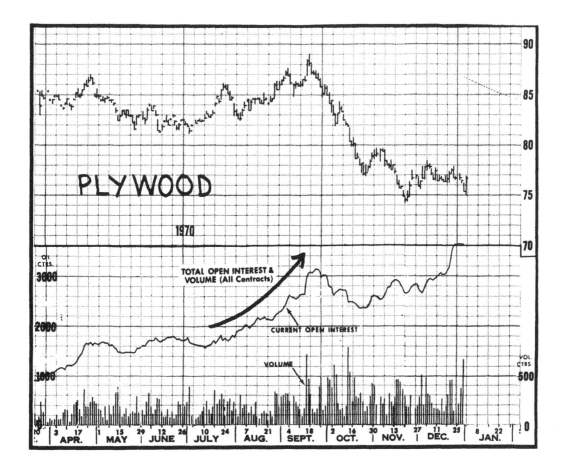

A good selling indication for Plywood was given in September 1970. For some six
months prices oscillated in a large trading range. Chartists saw this as a base for a
major advance. However, you would have known better because Open Interest
just kept climbing. Finally, as we expected, the market broke down.

Look at Silver in June and July of 1970. Here is a perfect example of the Open Interest buy indication. For two months prices were in a trading range, yet, the Open Interest plummeted, giving us clear-cut evidence that a rally was coming. And come it did.

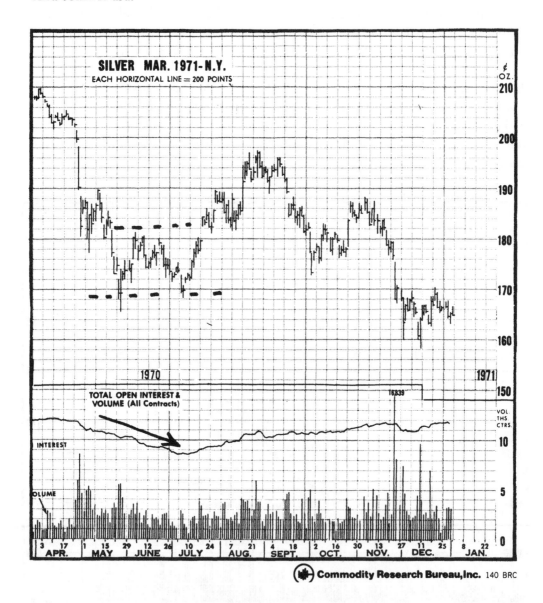

SILVER MAR. 1971- N.Y.
EACH HORIZONTAL LINE = 200 POINTS

TOTAL OPEN INTEREST & VOLUME (All Contracts)

INTEREST

VOLUME

(●) Commodity Research Bureau, Inc. 140 BRC

In July, August and September 1970, Soy Bean Oil was in a flat, to slightly higher trading range. Some of the most astute Bean Oil analysts were forecasting lower prices and a crash in the market. That never happened. Instead, a sizeable rally began.

What triggered or started the rally? Our trusty Open Interest figures. See how the line broke sharply, telling us the commercials were covering their shorts as fast as they could. Obviously, they knew the true fundamental picture was about to become more bullish.

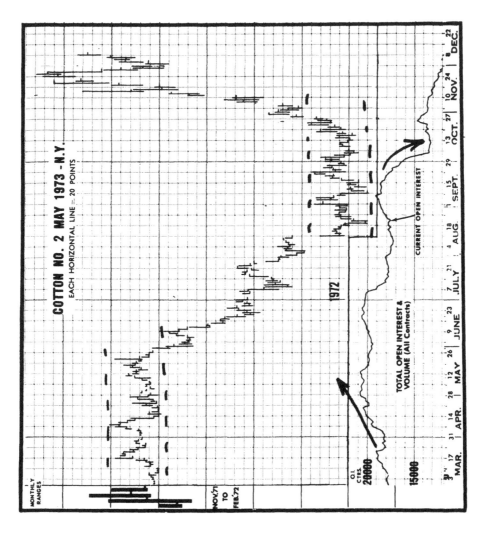

COTTON NO. 2 MAY 1973 - N.Y.

EACH HORIZONTAL LINE = 20 POINTS

TOTAL OPEN INTEREST & VOLUME (All Contracts)

CURRENT OPEN INTEREST

MONTHLY RANGES

NOV.'71 TO FEB.'72

1972

O.I. CTRS. 20000

15000

3¾ 17 | 31 14 | 28 12 26 | 9 23 | 7 21 | 4 18 | 1 15 | 29 | 13 27 | 10 24 | 8 22
MAR. | APR. | MAY | JUNE | JULY | AUG. | SEPT. | OCT. | NOV. | DEC.

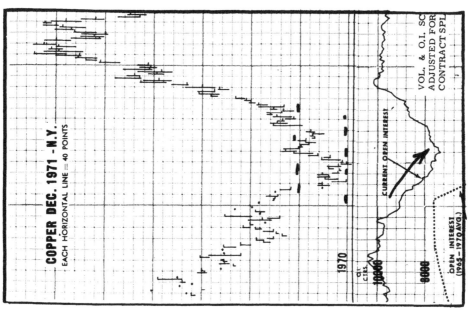

COPPER DEC. 1971 - N.Y.

EACH HORIZONTAL LINE = 40 POINTS

CURRENT OPEN INTEREST

VOL. & O.I. SC
ADJUSTED FOR
CONTRACT SPI

OPEN INTEREST
(1965 – 1970 AVG.)

1970

O.I. CTRS. 10000

8000

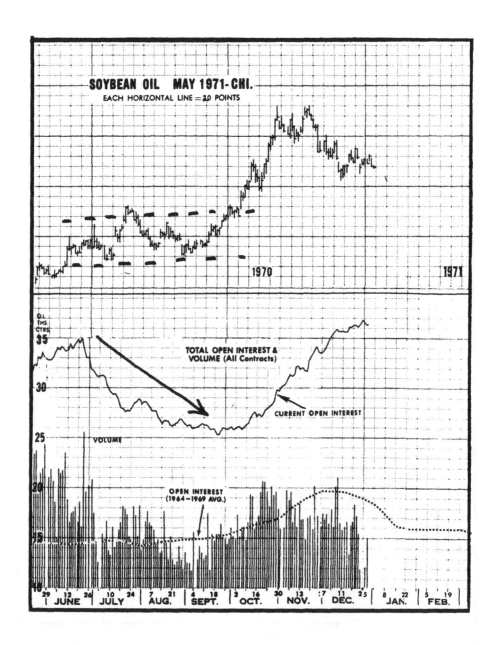

SOYBEAN OIL   MAY 1971- CHI.
EACH HORIZONTAL LINE = 20 POINTS

Copper works nicely with the Open Interest data. In January of 1971, Copper prices probed for a bottom in a trading range market. At that time, Open Interest had a drastic "peel off" telling us higher prices were most likely in order. Indeed they were because prices sailed from 44¢ to 59¢ in three months!

An excellent short selling indication was given in the Cotton market in 1972. During April and May, prices entered a trading range and open interest steadily increased thereby warning of an imminent market collapse.

And collapse it surely did!

58

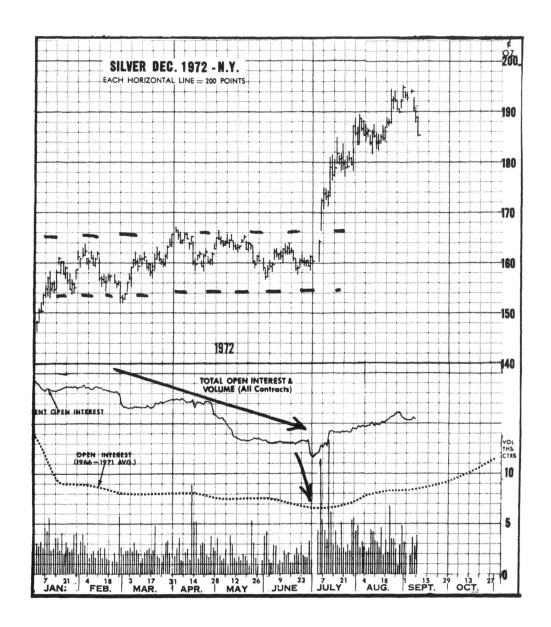

Silver began a sensational bull market in 1972. That's history, but at the time, the Silver bulls had just been flushed out of the market by an October slide. Search as you may — you could not find a Silver bull on the street. However, a few of us were able to position this market on the long side. Why? Because prices had intered a large trading range (as defined on the chart) while Open Interest steadily declined.

The handwriting was on the charts for all to see. Commercials had covered their shorts and the market was ready to explode.

And did it ever!

## WHY THESE MILLION DOLLAR TOOLS WORK

It's pleasant to sip fine cognac late at night and discuss the market's ups, downs, do's and don'ts. My learned college professor friends say the market is entirely unpredictable. I must agree. Much of the market's action defies forecasting and certainly, price action by itself, is not terribly predictive.

However, when we turn our attention away from price action to indications of the professional's doings, our system will usually work. Certainly, professionals occasionally get caught on the wrong side of the market. However, over any given length of time, the "pros" still come out winners. That's why the tools mentioned will make money for you. They deal with professional opinion, not price movements.

I'll continue to argue with college professors about just how random or non-random price action is, but let's keep in mind that it's my 45 year old cognac we're drinking!

## ADDITIONAL TOOLS TO "CLINCH" YOUR TRADES

### CONTRARY OPINION

If, at the time my million dollar tools are giving buy indications, most advisory services are going against my indications, your chances for a good trade are further increased! I mean this sincerely. As with the stock market, when too many people believe something will happen, it never does.

You can objectively measure contrary opinion by subscribing to Market Vane, (431 East Green Street, Pasadena, California) or by ordering Maduff & Sons (6399 Wilshire Boulevard, Los Angeles, California 90048), a weekly brokerage letter. Both sources will give you the per cent of services that are bullish or bearish in the commodity field. Invariably, as the services become 100% bullish, trend following, the market sells off. 15% to 30% bullish readings usually evidence a sizeable up move.

However, it is important that you use bullish readings that are under 30% only in markets that are in strong up trends. Sell signals, (50% to 100% bullish readings) are good in bear markets, but only so-so in bull markets.

### NEWS ACTION

If, at the same time my million dollar tools are saying "buy", a very bearish piece of news is released that has little effect on the market, you can rest assured that the tools are correct and a large up move will begin.

The 1973 Copper bull market was signaled in this fashion. Open Interest saw a sharp decline and the premium picture was improving. It was then announced that a large quantity of Copper was to be placed for sale on the market. This should have caused a limit down move — that's what was expected. Instead, prices sold off for two hours, then rallied, telling us this market was in very strong hands.

## HOW CHARTS FORECAST

I'll have more comments on chart action in another chapter, but for now, let me just say this: when prices begin gapping on your charts (see the example) this is an indication of intensified buying and selling. Gaps are usually found at the beginning of up moves. Gaps occurring after prices have been in a trading range usually indicate which way prices will break out of the trading range. Study the examples given here and you'll see what I mean.

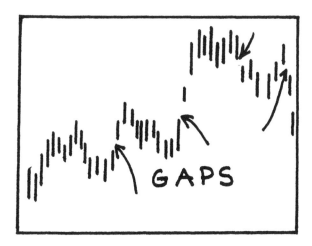

## COMMITMENT OF LARGE TRADERS

When you see a commodity wherein the large traders are overwhelmingly short or long, you are assured that, at some time in the future, prices should move in their favor. An ideal bullish situation is where the large traders are long, five contracts for every one they are short. For selling, they should be short five contracts for every one they are long.

As helpful as the large trader's report may be, it does have some drawbacks about which you should be informed. Much of the large trader activity reflects hedging, or spreading, and is due to seasonal crop tendencies. It can be misleading. Nonetheless, it is nice to back up an opinion derived from other data. Perhaps the report's greatest drawback is that it is issued only for the grains, meats and eggs.

## HOW TO IDENTIFY TREND DIRECTION

You've heard the old saying, "You can't fight City Hall", "Don't spit into the wind", or, "Buck the market". Well, they all mean the same thing. That's fine, but how are we to tell what the true underlying trend is?

I have no absolute answers. I've tried many systems, but I keep coming back to one very simple index which I'll discuss in the chapter on timing buys and sales. The index is simply, ten week moving average.

To construct it, you add the Friday close for the last ten weeks and divide by 10. Then, plot this on your chart. As long as the average is slanting upward, the underlying price trend is still up and we can buy without bucking the market.

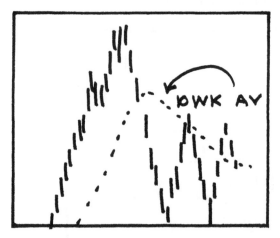

Should the ten week moving average line be trending down, I assume prices are headed lower. This means I sell short only if the 10 week moving average is down. I buy long only if it is up. It's a dandy tool to keep you out of bad trades and will help to further identify the 10 to 1 odds we've been striving for.

Identify the premium spreads and look for Open Interest increases or decreases during trading ranges. This is your main method for identifying where the next big bull or bear market will commence.

Then, substantiate this by checking contrary opinion, news action, large trader reports, gaps, and the trend direction.

Once you find a "deal" with an increasing premium and Open Interest decreasing during a trading range, you are ready to select your point of entry. The tools discussed above are not for timing your buy or sell. They are tools for selecting the commodities on which you should concentrate your energies. Don't expect these tools to do more than that or you'll be headed for big trouble.

Market timing is discussed in the next chapter.

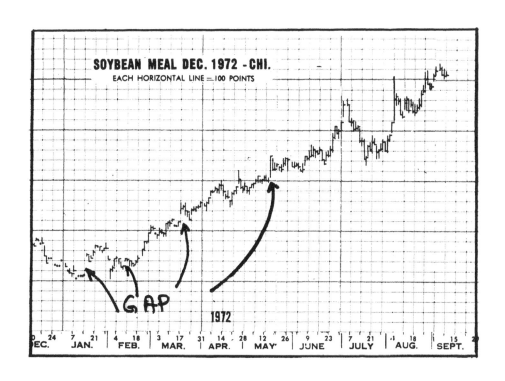

SOYBEAN MEAL DEC. 1972 - CHI.
EACH HORIZONTAL LINE = 100 POINTS

GAP

1972

DEC. | JAN. | FEB. | MAR. | APR. | MAY | JUNE | JULY | AUG. | SEPT.

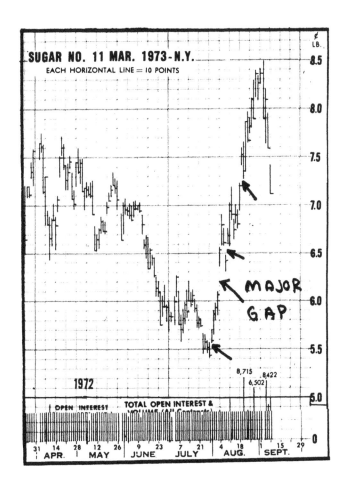

SUGAR NO. 11 MAR. 1973-N.Y.
EACH HORIZONTAL LINE = 10 POINTS

¢ LB.
8.5
8.0
7.5
7.0
6.5
6.0
5.5
5.0

MAJOR GAP

1972

8,715
6,502
8,422

OPEN INTEREST    TOTAL OPEN INTEREST & VOLUME (All Contracts)

0

31 | 14 | 28 | 12 | 26 | 9 | 23 | 7 | 21 | 4 | 18 | 1 | 15 | 29
APR. | MAY | JUNE | JULY | AUG. | SEPT.

# CHAPTER SIX

## MY MILLION DOLLAR — NEVER BEFORE REVEALED — TRADING TOOLS

# MY MILLION DOLLAR — NEVER BEFORE REVEALED — TRADING TOOLS

By this time you should have learned the basics of the commodity market, money management, and an understanding of yourself as well as how a successful trader thinks. Additionally, and of great importance, you have been told how to scout out the big trades, the sure-thing deals on which you will concentrate your energies.

It is now time to give you the final touches enabling you to time your points of entry into and exit from the commodity markets.

At the risk of being redundant, I want to make certain you understand how vitally important it is to select good trades.

This chapter will perhaps, be the most interesting of all to you traders. The tools I am about to discuss may not have been brought to your attention previously. They will be profitable only if used in conjunction with the well-defined, major bull and bear market moves. Should you choose to use these indices on the sloppy, go-no-where markets, or markets that are not tightly locked in (where future direction is questionable) forget about their effectiveness.

I suspect this might lead some readers to become angry with me, but I want you to know that you have my sincere wish for market success and that success will come only if you confine your efforts, using technical tools, for the well-defined markets.

## A WORD ON TECHNICAL THEORY

Technical tools rely on daily price action as opposed to the underlying fundamentals. In view of this fact, one must be cognizant of the knowledge that such tools are subject to rapid and unforeseeable changes. The trader that changes with the tools will make money. The trader who gets trapped by a bad signal, but keeps hoping for the good one to re-materialize, will be hurt. All technical tools are subject to whip-saw action. All technical tools can be in error. Even my million dollar tools are wrong from time to time. But, by and large, they are correct and their performance is further improved when they are used for the well-defined markets.

There are three basic approaches upon which all technical tools are based. The most common technical approach is a trend method. Then there's the momentum method, the over-sold/over-bought method, and finally, work based on the amount of accumulation and distribution taking place in the market.

Trend approaches are most apt to give false signals and stunning losses. As a matter of fact, during the past two weeks' market activity, a commodity trend system (probably the most widely followed), lost 40% of their equity. In one day, their accounts were down over 17%!

The trend approach works well in long term, sustainable trends. However, when trading ranges develop, any trading system (such as penetrations of any moving average, point and figure) will result in losses. To my knowledge, no one has yet constructed a profitable trend-following program that makes money every year.

The essence of the problem is that trend systems cannot forecast which markets will have the long, sustainable moves that make trend following profitable. Trend systems do not forecast, they merely identify.

## THE PROFITABILITY OF MOMENTUM

My concept of momentum, (bandied about by many other services, books, and brokerage firms) is based on measuring the speed at which prices advance and decline.

Imagine, for a moment, a ball being tossed into the air. At some point, the very untrained eye can say the ball will now begin falling because we can see the speed of travel has begun to diminish. And so it is with commodities with the exception that it takes a highly trained eye to detect this loss of momentum toward either an up or down movement.

To simplify, or define the speed, or rate of travel for prices, I devised the use of price rate-of-change about five years ago. My definition and tools for measuring speed are quite elementary. Compared to the machinations of my computerized predecessors, my methods are downright child's play.

The momentum concept shown here will be as accurate as any of which I am aware. Best of all it's the simplest to maintain on a daily basis. Here's how it's done:

## HOW FAST ARE PRICES CHANGING?

Finding out the rate at which a commodity's prices are changing is not difficult. It takes only a few seconds per commodity, and all you need is some paper and a couple of sharp pencils.

Let's say, for example, that you wanted to construct a 25-day rate of change index for August 1972 pork-belly prices. To get today's index number, you subtract the closing price 25 days ago from today's closing price. If bellies closed at 38.44 then and 38.72 today, today's index number would be 38.72 minus 38.44 — or .28. (You always subtract 25 days ago from today. If bellies closed at 38.44 then and at 38.02 today, the index number would be — .38.) Tomorrow you would do the same, using tomorrow's closing price and that of 25 days earlier. That would give you your next index number. And so on.

These index numbers are plotted chronologically above or below a "zero-line" on a graph with an appropriate scale. They are then connected with a solid line, as shown on the bottom of the accompanying chart for August '72 bellies, to form a momentum curve.

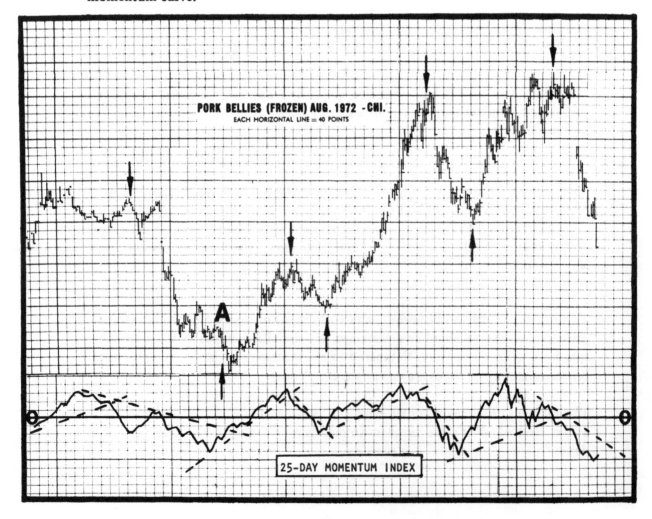

PORK BELLIES (FROZEN) AUG. 1972 -CHI.
EACH HORIZONTAL LINE = 40 POINTS

25-DAY MOMENTUM INDEX

66

There's more to the momentum curve than may meet your eye. A rising curve means an increase in upward momentum — if it's above the zero line. A rising curve below the zero line signifies a decrease in downward momentum. By the same token, a falling curve means an increase in downward momentum below the zero line, a decrease in upward momentum above the zero line.

Once the curve is constructed, there are many ways it may be used to help you forecast prices. A simple but relatively effective way involves drawing trend lines on the curve itself, as shown on the chart. Although momentum generally tops or bottoms out well in advance of prices, the best signals come when long-term trends of the momentum index are broken. Point A on the chart provides a good example, as the downtrend in momentum was penetrated well ahead of the market turn.

Another approach is to construct a 10-day moving average of the momentum index itself, taking it as a "buy" signal when the momentum index crosses above its own 10-day moving average, as a "sell" signal when it falls below it.

## TIME PERIOD IMPORTANT

It was not by chance that 25 days was used in the example above. Most commodities exhibit some degree of cyclical price behavior. The momentum principle works better when an effort is made to match the time period used to the harmonics of the particular market concerned. In pork bellies, the cycle — the number of days from bottom to bottom — is about 50. Therefore, 25 days — or one-half of the cycle's time span — was chosen as the basis for calculating our rate-of-change or momentum index.

## THE MARKETS' MOST IMPORTANT TECHNICAL ASPECT

For my money, the technical theory of most value and validity is the concept of overbought/oversold. This theory, or concept, is indeed the basis for all life and all thought. Let's turn our attention to nature, or the human body, to get a better grasp of this, the most important technical concept.

In nature, we have light and dark. Night and day. For direction, we have north and south. Within our own frame of reference we have feelings of joy or sorrow. We are hot or cold, and even our body chemistry is either alkaline or acidic. Indeed, all things in nature are based on the underlying concept of opposites. Front and back, sweet and sour. As the Chinese would have it . . . Yin and Yang.

As readers of my previous book are aware, I'm quite involved in the Yin and Yang philosophy, especially as it relates to the markets. The original concept, founded by the Chinese many thousands of years ago, is simply that there are two forces in the world by which everything may be defined.

The interworkings of these forces is that Yin, just about begins to overtake and completely dominate Yang, the opposite force. Then, Yang regains its strength, refurbishes its power and begins to conquer Yin when Yin, once more, re-develops its strength. And so it goes, a never ending battle of good and evil, light and dark, hot and cold, or overbought and oversold.

Strangely enough, within Yang there is some Yin and within Yin there is some Yang. Just as we find some good in the most evil person, some bad in all saints, some light in what at first seems a dark room.

My observation of market action has revealed to me that just as a condition of price imbalance appears to be a one way street, the opposite force takes over. What looked like a sure thing is soon falling out of bed. That's why traders who buy on break outs don't last very long.

A break out condition usually occurs at the tail end of a move when buyers are in almost total domination of sellers. That condition, according to Yin and Yang, can't last long.

I'm certain you've seen what I'm talking about. As sellers become so strong, so certain of themselves, they must be defeated as buyers rise up to take advantage of the imbalance.

Perhaps the key to technical study is understanding balance and imbalance. I have done some work along those lines that has been encouraging but not quite enough to report to you at this time.

## HOW TO TELL WHEN A COMMODITY IS OVERSOLD

Enough about concepts and abstracts. Here, exactly, is how I identify an overbought or oversold market.

My method may, or may not be the ultimate answer to Yin and Yang. However, it is the best I have found considering the irrational character of price action and the ease of constructing the index. As an additional bonus, the index is done on a % basis so you know exactly the nature of an extreme. Overbought/oversold indices that use only the price range from one point to another have no absolutes. Thusly, what was oversold at one time period may not be oversold at another.

I'll refer to the index as % of R, or %R. The index is a simple measure of where today's closing price fits within the total Range of the last ten days.

Let's say the range for the last ten days was ten points, with the highest high of the last ten days at 65, and the lowest low of the last ten days at 55.

Today's closing price is 58. As you can see from the illustration the close is quite low, within context of the total range during the last ten days.

In terms of percentages, the close at 58 represents a figure that is 70% of the total range.

Should the commodity have closed at 55, the % would be 100%. That is, the close is 100% of the distance from the top of the range to the close. If prices had closed at 65, the % reading would have been 0 because the distance from the close is 0% of the distance from the high to the close.

The exact formula for arriving at %R is first to determine the distance from the highest high of the past ten days and the lowest low of the last ten days. This is the "Range".

Then, take the difference from the high of the last ten days, which you have already identified, and today's closing price. We'll call this "Change".

All that's left to do is divide the Change figure by the Range figure and you will arrive at what % today's price is — out of the last ten day's range. It's as simple as that. Here's an example. Let's say Silver had a high of 280.5 the last ten days and a low of 272.5. Today's close is 278.5. The Range (high to low) is 80. The Change (today's close to 10 day high) is 20. When we divide 20 by 80 we arrive at what % today's closing level represents of the total ten day range. In this case, the %R reading is 25%.

Plot this daily reading on your chart paper. It will, naturally, range from a Yang, (overbought reading at 0%) to Yin, (an oversold reading at 100%). Generally speaking, readings below 95% give a buy indication — during bull markets. A reading above 10% gives a sell signal during bear markets.

The preceeding paragraph is the essence of my technical system. The %R index will not work if you insist on acting on the buy signals during a bear market. Now you realize why I have, in earlier chapters, stressed so strongly, the necessity of isolating the dominant bull and bear markets. Once you've done that, all you have to do is track price movements with %R and wait for the signals telling you it's time to start positioning the commodity according to the fundamental situation we have discussed.

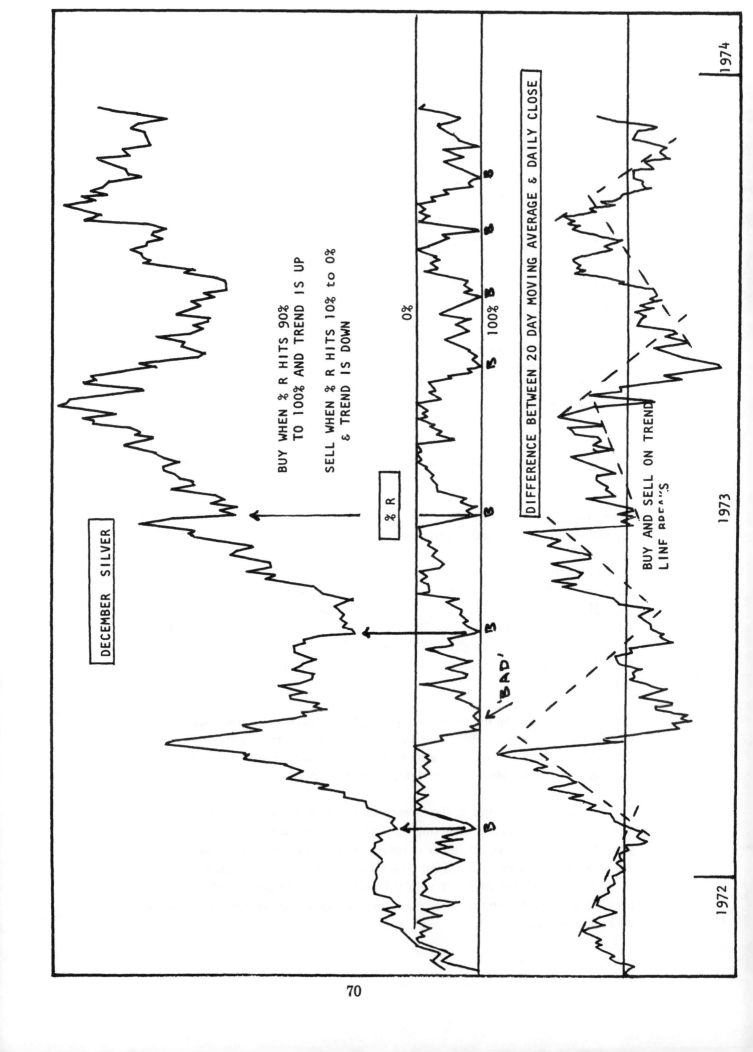

DECEMBER SILVER

BUY WHEN % R HITS 90%
TO 100% AND TREND IS UP

SELL WHEN % R HITS 10% to 0%
& TREND IS DOWN

0%

% R

100%

DIFFERENCE BETWEEN 20 DAY MOVING AVERAGE & DAILY CLOSE

BUY AND SELL ON TREND
LINE BREAKS

'BAD'

1972        1973        1974

Let's review some examples of %R at work to see its limitations as well as its advantages and historical record. As you will see, it always calls the best buy and sell areas. This is a dandy index.

## TIMING YOUR SILVER TRADES

Here's a chart of December Silver starting on November 17, 1972 through November 1, 1973. During this period, silver was in a well-identified bull market as I repeatedly indicated in my advisory service at the time. This means our interest in the %R index was strictly on the buy side. The signals we would "work" were those given by %R dropping below 95%. In total, eight signals were given. All predicted immediate rallies of at least a full cent. That's a $1,000 profit per contract.

There is one "bad" period which I've been careful to mark on this chart. This is an example of when %R signals can go haywire. This is the only screening you have to make on a buy signal in a bull market.

If prices have recently undergone an extremely rapid rise, exhibiting signs of a technical blow-off, (that means prices will stage a wild, upside move then immediately limit down without trading) wait for a buy signal from the %R Index. You are through waiting and ready to buy, when:

1. %R has hit 100%,
2. Five trading days have passed since the 100% reading was hit,
3. %R again falls below 95%.

Once those three criteria are met, it's time to once again begin acting on the %R signals, assuming you are buying long in a bull market.

Unless there has been a wild, speculative blow-off in the bull market, you should try to position every time the index falls below 95%. This procedure assures that you are buying on extreme weakness at a time Yang is about to overtake Yin.

Not all signals will be correct. I have constructed no perfect indices. The Holy Grail is yet to be found. Because of that, I use a few other tools to confirm the %R and I use stops as my ultimate protection. Yet, %R remains the best timing tool I have ever used for determining overbought or oversold markets.

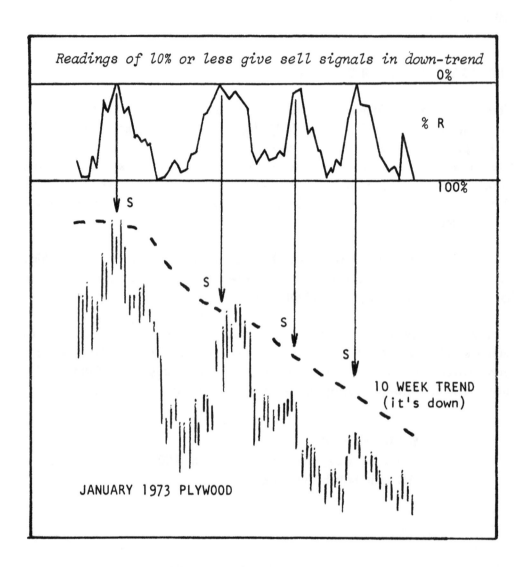

Readings of 10% or less give sell signals in down-trend

0%

% R

100%

S

S

S

S

10 WEEK TREND
(it's down)

JANUARY 1973 PLYWOOD

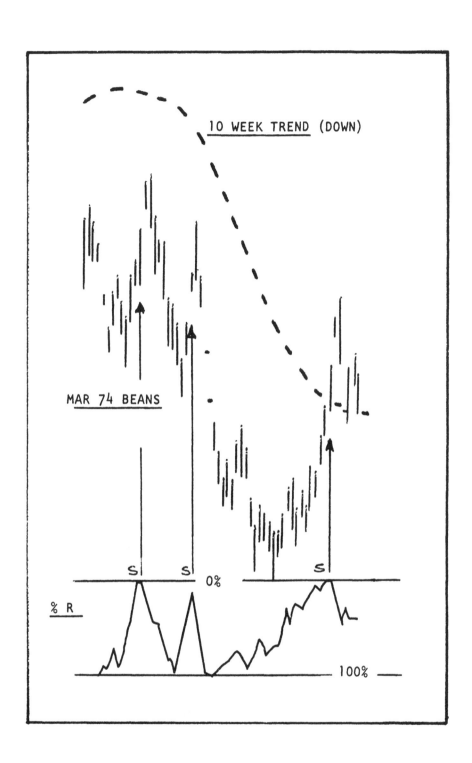

10 WEEK TREND (DOWN)

MAR 74 BEANS

% R

S    S    0%    S

100%

SOY BEAN OIL AND SUPER PROFITS

During 1973, Soy Bean Oil was also in an easy-to-identify bull market. Open Interest had several huge reductions. A premium appeared and large traders were long. All signs were "go". It was only a question of selecting optimum times to buy. Enter, %R!

In the ten month chart of Bean Oil prices, ten signals were given by %R as I have marked on the chart. All but one of the signals was followed by immediate and substantial gains. That's not bad! Alert chartists will notice the signals come when prices are extremely weak. Thus, you are almost always able to buy into massive weakness . . . not after a turn has developed.

Indeed, that's the beauty of the index. While most gauges wait for a turn to develop, %R identifies the exact low point, give or take a day. This means, you can wait until after the signal is given — no need to trade during market hours — and place your order for the following morning open when prices are on the skids following through the previous day's liquidation. That's a humdinger of a time to take down large, large positions.

## THE SECRET OF SELLING SHORT

We reverse our procedures for selling short with %R. We look for a well-defined bear market. That means, prices have been trending lower; Open Interest is on the increase, there are no premiums and the nearby months are weaker than the distant.

Our next move is to wait for %R to zoom up to 10% or less. Notice the beautiful sell signals given in Plywood during the 1973 market period (Yes, Virginia, there were bear markets).

At this point, Yin is about to overtake Yang and market traders begin selling to the newcomers. Here, the exact day of the high was called quite well by %R. The index has a great ability to call our attention to many major selling levels in bear markets.

## IDENTIFYING A SELLING POINT FOR BEANS

In September, 1973 Soy Beans were in a well-identified bear trend. A quick glance at the chart makes that quite clear. The alert trader was ready to sell short. The question was, when, and could %R spot the selling time?

74

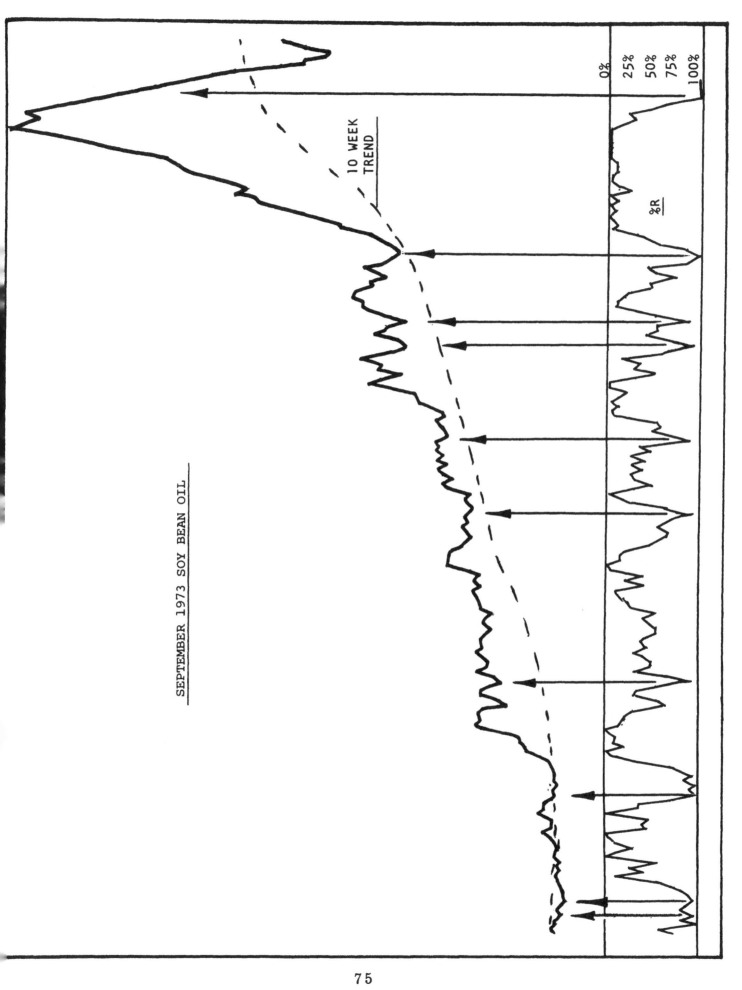

SEPTEMBER 1973 SOY BEAN OIL

10 WEEK TREND

%R

0%
25%
50%
75%
100%

It did in sterling fashion. The tool raised to 11% telling us it was time to short. The next day it was limit up and we had our sell signal at 680. The following day it was all over. Beans took a dive down to the 590 area. Had you sold one contract at 680 and covered at 590, on a margin of $3,000, you would have had a net gain of over $4,000 just ten days later!

Your bear market strategy using %R will be to wait until Open Interest has had a sizeable increase (while prices remain in the bear market), and then %R hits the selling area at 10% or less. The final indication that you should pull the trigger comes the day after %R gives the sell signal.

Let 'em have it with both barrels. Place your stop, walk away. Your work is done for the time being!

## HOW TO HANDLE TRADING RANGES

Most technical systems are butchered during trading ranges. How about %R? Well, as a matter of record, it was designed to help me as it identified the tops and lows of trading range markets with explicit exactness.

March 1973 Sugar is a good example of an extended trading range market. My work gave convincing evidence prices would go higher. Yet, in a trading range, a buy and hold strategy is not as successful as a buy and sell policy.

During such situations you buy when the %R hits 90% or lower. Sell and short when it bounces back into the 10% range. You will find an amazing degree of correlation between trading range tops and %R peaks. Ditto for bottoms.

Trading ranges mean prices are locked into supply on the topside and demand, underneath. Usually, supply comes in with a high %R reading and demand returns when %R falls back to the low buy area.

Several other examples of %R are shown here for your study and observation. Their greatest value will be for your historical perspective. Study them, refer to them. You should have a better feel for the index when you develop information on the commodities you wish to follow.

## HOW TO COMBINE MOMENTUM WITH %R

You now have an understanding of momentum, overbought, and oversold. It's time to synthesize the two. While I have told you to explicitly use the ten day basis for %R in the measurement of momentum, there are other time periods to use such as twenty-five days, etc. Choose whichever seems to be working best based on the current cycles. That's the key to momentum — extracting the correct time period — then using the momentum approach.

That's what I do. Yet, people are always asking me for a uniform time period in which to work. Unfortunately, there isn't any. But, if I'm really pressed, I tell people that a twenty day period is optimum, especially if they take a twenty-day moving average of price and then determine how far above or below that average is today's price.

The math is easy. Take the last twenty days' closing prices and divide by twenty. Then take the difference by which today's closing price is greater or lesser than this twenty day figure. This difference will oscillate above and below a line that represents uniformity in price or zero difference.

The Silver chart shown here indicates several good buy and sell gain signals from the momentum gauge. The signals are generated by a long term break in the momentum trend line. When that occurs it tells us prices have lost their power and a trend reversal is in gear. Get ready!


## HOW TO USE THESE TOOLS IN A BULL MARKET

In a well-defined bull market you will be buying on a %R signal at, for example, "A" on the Silver chart. Your sell is given when the long term trend on momentum tops out as defined by a trend line ("B" on the chart).

In this case there was a $5,500 gain for every $1,000 invested.

The trick here is to use the %R data for entering the market and the momentum trends for exiting. A final hint: when the momentum figure becomes extreme, by historical comparison, it's time to cover your position without waiting for the trend reversal to take place. There is nothing wrong with taking profits in advance of a trend reversal in momentum . . . especially if the index is at an extreme level. Remember . . . Yin and Yang.


## HOW TECHNICAL DATA CAN IDENTIFY THE FUNDAMENTALS

Here is an index that's so simple you'd almost be inclined to scoff at it. But consider . . . it will enable you to have a clear-cut fundamental view of any market, at any time. This little tool is one of the secrets of my advisory service, Commodity Timing.

First, let's visualize the market and determine why we have bullish or bearish trends. Such trends develop because the fundamentals dictate a bear trend and because enough traders, who are aware of the fundamentals, are selling and pushing prices down. Reverse the procedures for causes of a bull market.

77

I have concluded that it is impossible to always know the underlying fundamentals. It's beyond my comprehension. All I can do, at best, is isolate markets where the odds are in my favor. In markets where I have no "feel" for the fundamentals, I turn to price structure to learn the fundamentals.

After all, if fundamentals cause price trends, price trends can tell us what the fundamentals may be.

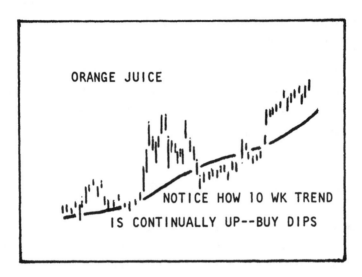

The problem is in determining exactly what the price trend is. How can we do this? Isn't it true that the markets are far too erratic to arrive accurately at the overall trend?

I really don't think so. I can always tell you the probable future direction of prices (the fundamentals) by taking a ten week moving average of the Friday closes. That is, all Friday closes for the last ten weeks. Scoot your decimal point over one digit and you have the ten week average.

## TEN WEEK AVERAGE · · · · RULES

1. Assume the commodity is bullish and expect higher prices if, and only if, the ten week moving average is going upward.
2. Assume the commodity is bearish and expect lower prices if, and only if, the ten week moving average is headed down.
3. Assume the fundamentals are unknown and a trading range will persist if, and only if, the ten week moving average is flat. If there is a bias to be given, it would be in favor of the 10 week trend prior to going flat.

78

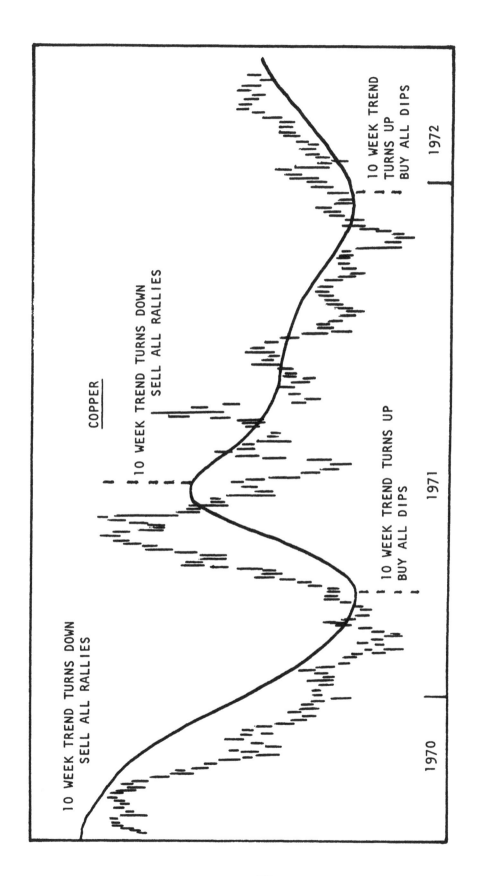

## HOW PRICE SMOOTHING DETECTS THE TRUE TREND

When you run a ten week moving average you smooth out all the fluctuations in price action. By doing this, you can develop a smooth line indicating the underlying trend. Elementary physics tell us that once a force is set in motion, that trend persists. We know we have a reliable tool to help us see the price structure.

MARCH 1973 SUGAR

ACTION LOOKS LIKE A TRADING RANGE
BUT 10 WK TREND SAYS BUY ALL DIPS

Allow me to interject at this point; the ten week trend method works best on commodities — not stocks. One needs other tools for stocks.

## HOW TO USE THE FUNDAMENTAL DIRECTION INDEX

Now that you have constructed the ten week moving average, you have isolated fundamentals. You have a key, and some insight to the future. As long as the line is slanting upwards on your charts, you should work only the long side of the market. When the line goes flat, you will go long and short on %R signals, and when the line heads downward, you will work just the short side of the market.

Should you choose to buck the ten week line, remember you are bucking the underlying fundamental strengths of the market. Why do it!

The examples here will give you a pretty fair idea of the workings of a ten week trend line. Notice that what appears to be a sloppy market in Wheat and Oil were actually fundamentally strong, telling the trader to be a buyer on the big pullbacks.

## A NEGATIVE NOTE

While the ten week trend method is quite good, we must keep in mind that its purpose is not timing our optimum selection. Its purpose is to point out the bullish and bearish markets. Crossing of price above or below this line have absolutely no bearing or significance. It is the <u>trend</u> of this line that is meaningful.

Also keep in mind that the index is always correct during moves but will never call a top or bottom. That's the function of the shorter term tools.

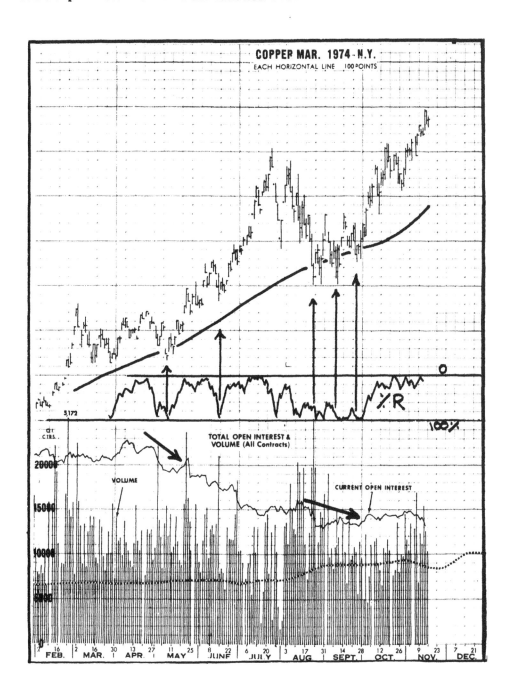

## WHAT A "LEAD-PIPE-CINCH" TRADE LOOKS LIKE

Using and combining the various fundamental indices about which I've talked, let's refer to Copper during August and September, 1973.

Observe: 1) the big decline in Open Interest, 2) the bullish price premium (October Copper was at 89¢, December, 83¢ and January, 81¢), 3) nearby Coppers gaining on distants                    and 4) the ten week trend is flat to up.

For timing purposes, two %R buy signals were given right at the lows. This is an example of a trade where the odds are overwhelmingly in your favor.

This is the longest chapter in the book. However, it may not be the most important to you. The chapter on money management or the one on transactional analysis may be the key to your success in the market. Regardless of which chapter you find most helpful I believe this one will require your most astute attention and, if you are like most of us, will demand a number of readings in order for you to thoroughly comprehend and absorb the material. Once you have developed a working feel for all the indicators, and have a good grasp of the indices, you will be primed and ready to begin trading.

# CHAPTER SEVEN

## HOW I READ CHARTS

## CHAPTER 7

### HOW I READ CHARTS

By and large, I am not impressed with chartists and their wiggly-waggly patterns that supposedly spell instant wealth. Chart readers have no concpet of probability, nor can they offer any valid reason (excuse) why their method should work. The only successful market system is one based on a practical, common sense, theory of why prices move. Chart systems are based on whims.

At best the chartist will say his flying wedges work because they reflect supply and demand in the market. That could be true. However, other sets of data — non-supply/demand based — produce the same supply/demand patterns. The number of traffic deaths in New York City will give great head and shoulder formations. Flip a penny and plot the runs of heads and tails, in point and figure fashion and you'll have something that looks just like a stock. Thus, how can charts show supply/demand patterns?

### WHAT CHARTS CAN SHOW

I do believe charts can give a broad view of market action in three ways. The first is that bull and bear markets tend to follow the same basic pattern just as the Green Bay Packers play pretty much the same game of football every week. Secondly, by using charts on a comparative basis, you can spot the strongest commodity within a complex or within a group of commodities. Thirdly, chart action can help identify turning points and starting points for sizeable moves.

I know of no way that charts will enable you to trade every swing of the market. Chart action is not a panacea for profits. At best it isolates situations where the odds are more in our favor, but does not mean it will always call the best trades or the best time to make our commitments.

### HOW CHARTS DETECT THE STRONGEST COMMODITY OR GROUP OF COMMODITIES

The majority of our selection problems will be taken care of by the fundamental tools we've already reviewed. But, from time to time, you will still have selection problems because you are bullish on a commodity but don't know which contract to buy. Or, you may be bullish on all grains, meats, etc., but want to select the one or two that should perform the best. Here's how to do it.

Small speculators and brokerage firm crap shooters insist on getting into the commodity contracts furthest away from delivery — the distant months. At times, this is correct. Usually, it is a fallacy. Charts can tell us which contracts we should be in when we use them on a comparative basis.

Let's say we are interested in buying Wheat. Our next step is to look closely at all the Wheat contracts being traded to see if one contract has been acting more strongly than the rest. This means we look for several developments, such as:

1.  Has one commodity refused to break a low that another commodity has fallen through?

2.  Has one commodity held its gains better than the rest of the group?

3.  Has one commodity shown a tendency to rally more; to have wider daily ranges?

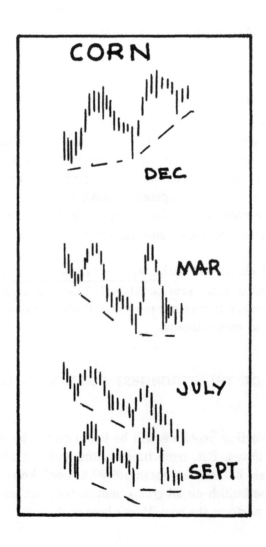

84

By keeping these questions in mind we will be able to see which commodity has been the strongest. That is, the month we'll want to buy with our signal. Such a situation in Corn is shown here. There are four different contracts all of the same time period. Which one should you buy when the time is right?

Hopefully, you said December Corn. It _has_ been the strongest because it held its gains better, and continually outperformed the other contracts. Not all examples will be this clear cut. It requires close study to perfect this technique, but it is invaluable. The successful trader must develop the art.

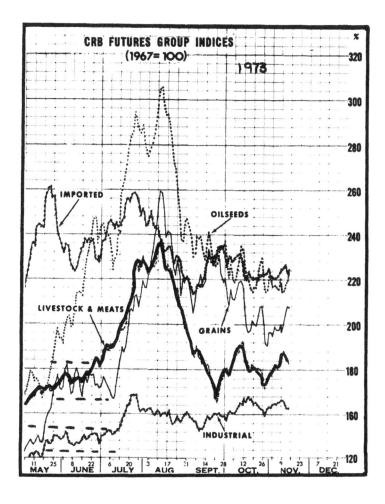

You can use this same technique to scout out the groups of commodities that should perform the best when it looks as though the entire market is about to take off.

Notice the trading range through which grains passed in mid-1973. In the meantime, meat prices were inching up telling us when the next phase of the bull market would resume and the dynamite would explode in the meat complex. Explode it did!

Along with subscribing to Commodity Research Bureau Chart Service, I also maintain charts. I usually have two or three options of each commodity that I follow. If at all possible, I chart them, one on top of the other, so I can more readily see the comparative strength of each contract. This is a valuable tool, full of insight to the markets. Treasure it.

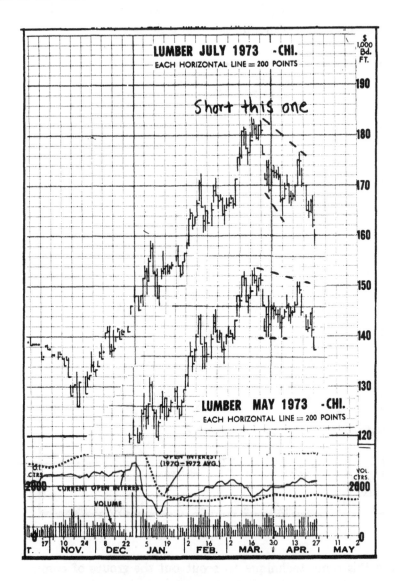

Comparative chart action is one of the most valuable tools I possess for analyzing the market activity on a day-to-day basis.

The following charts should help you get a better handle for "reading" them the way I do. Where appropriate I have made comments or placed trend lines, etc. to call your attention to the important divergences. It is this divergence from the rest of the pack that spots super strong, or weak commodities.

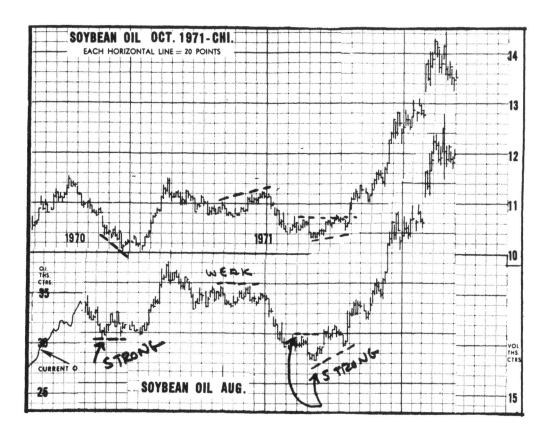

I have also shown examples of weak commodities in strong groups. These are the ones you want to sell when it's time to short.

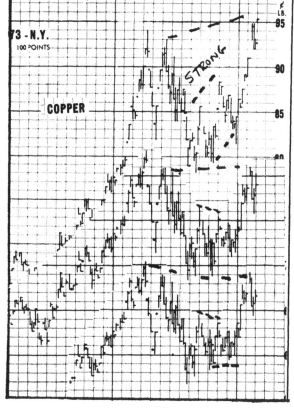

## HOW CHARTS IDENTIFY TURNING POINTS

To an extent, your charts will help you isolate days that see an up or down trend reverse. They will also help put you back on the track of the major trend. Such reversal days are seen in one of two fashions.

The most common reversal day is simply one where prices sell off substantially, almost always down limit, only to reverse and close up for the day. Such a day appears in the following diagram.

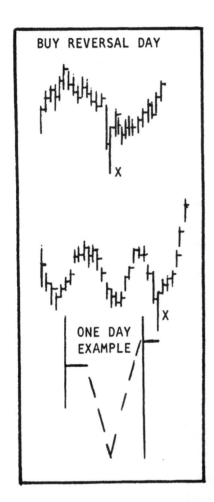

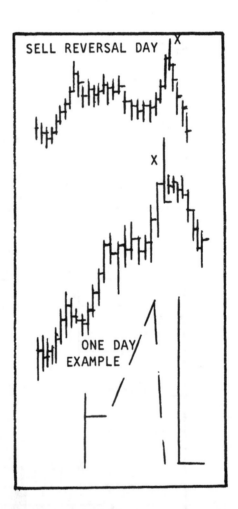

A series of top and bottom reversals are also shown for your observation. Notice, in each case, how a temporary reaction against the main trend was ended when we had the "flush-out" day with prices selling off drastically, then recovering, to close up for the day.

A reversal day is even more significant the longer the correction has been in effect.

## MY NEW REVERSAL DAY DISCOVERY

Our second form of reversal day, and one I'll bet you've never even heard about, starts with prices heading sharply lower and closing, sharply lower. Prices might end up limit down, or just "off sharply" but, in any event, prices take a beating and are down handsomely for the day.

The trend reversal is indicated the next morning when prices open a good deal higher than the previous day's close. Such unusual strength is indicative of a key reversal for the market. What happens, in essence, is that prices fail to follow through with the previous day's slide. This type of action is most unusual since lower prices forecast lower openings about 85% of the time. Lower prices, with substantially higher openings, are a "sure thing" that a new move has begun.

It is particularly significant if prices close down the limit, and the next day open slightly up. Limit moves should beget more limit moves. A reversal of this pattern points to a market opportunity.

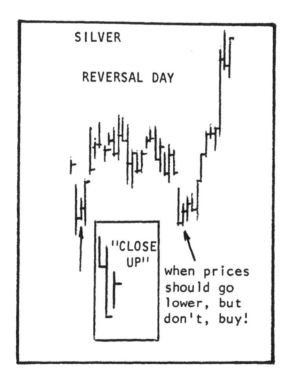

A special point of interest here is that an extremely strong signal is generated any time you have two reversal days with the second one higher, for a buy, lower for a sale. This is an unusual display of strength. I cannot recall when such a signal did not produce profits.

## THE MEANING OF GAPS

Gaps in price action, (when today's low is higher than yesterday's close; or today's high is lower than yesterday's close) can also signify important market moves.

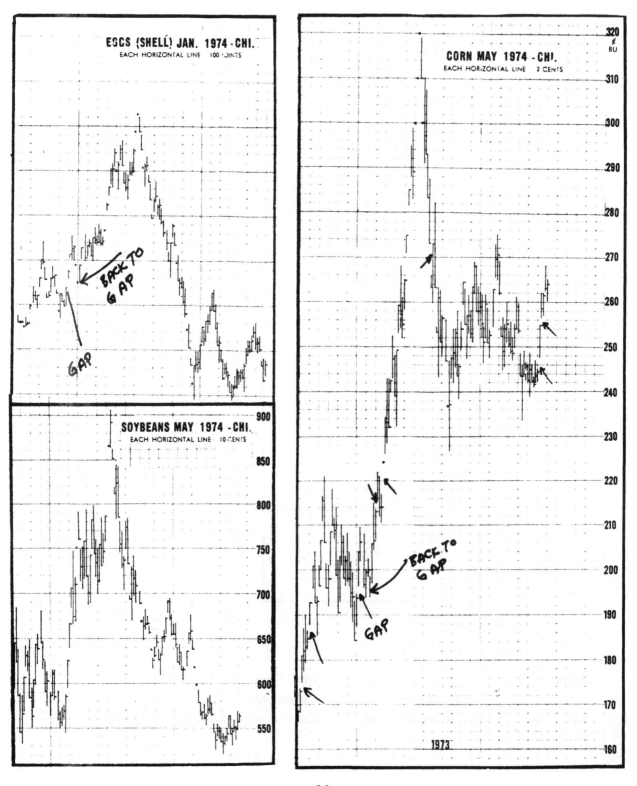

A gap in price is caused by a rush of buyers or sellers. Such displays of activity can forecast important moves on one, and only one basis.

If prices have been in a trading range, by looking for gaps you can usually foretell in which direction prices will come out of that trading range. If the gaps have been upside, (closes that are followed by lows higher than the close) prices will most likely move to the upside. The 1973 Corn chart shows many examples of this. The astute trader would have noticed many, many gaps — almost all to the upside — during trading ranges and consolidations — thereby foretilling higher prices.

Our rule here then, is that prices move out of trading areas in the direction of the most, or largest gaps.


## HOW GAPS HELP YOU GET DISCOUNTED PRICES

Since gaps reflect an imbalance of activity, prices usually spurt upward and then come back into the gap area. This does not always happen, but if you are trying to purchase a commodity, a logical place to buy under the market, is in the middle of the gap.

At times, these gaps act almost magically, drawing prices right into the gap area. The most typical buy and sell gap filling activity is shown here. Notice how it embodies the large move in the direction of the gap, then a pull back to the gap area before the main trend is resumed.

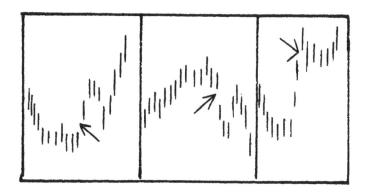

By waiting for prices to be sucked back to the gap you are able to buy quite a bit lower — at a discount — compared to people who bought a day or two following the gap day.

Again, I'm presenting several actual examples with comments, lines and arrows to give you a working understanding of how to handle gaps.

# CHAPTER EIGHT




## THE GREAT SILVER SECRET

CHAPTER 8

THE GREAT SILVER SECRET

This is the fun chapter of my book because I'm about to expose you to something you probably won't believe; something most people laugh at when I first broach the subject. Then I'll proceed to show you, which at first seems laughable, but is indeed a highly accurate method of forecasting the moves of certain commodities . . . months in advance!

I'd better get this off my chest. I believe that one can, with amazing accuracy, forecast the markets by using . . . the moon!

When Burton Pugh penned a little pamphlet called The Great Wheat Secret some fifty years ago, the reaction went from "Bah, Humbug", to "Amazing". The pamphlet was indeed amazing — it sold for $30.00! And back in 1930 that was a whole month's groceries. However, it did offer an unusually reliable method for trading in the grain markets and this method was based on buying during a full moon and selling during a new moon. Crazy, huh?

I suspect few traders took Pugh seriously, but today, our minds are a bit more receptive to different trading approaches and certainly, anyone who is familiar with the moon's effect on earth's existence will not scoff at Pugh's early writings.

While most of us know the moon revolves around the earth every 28 days and the moon's energies cause tides to rise and lower as much as sixty feet, few are aware that psychologists have discovered all humans have within their emotional framework a specific cycle of ups and downs. This cycle evolves through a period of twenty-eight days.

Market buffs are surprised to learn their favorite cycles are tied directly to the moon's actions. Any serious student of market cycles knows the most dominant stock cycles are the nine, seventeen and thirty-seven year cycles.

Did you know that our friend, the man-in-the-moon makes one complete cycle (one revolution of the moon, within its orbit) every 8.85 years. That creates the popular nine year cycle. Doubling that 8.85 figure gives us the popular seventeen year cycle!

The most important long term market cycle, according to my research, is based on a thirty-seven year count. Example: adding thirty-seven years to 1929 gives us 1966! Ironically enough, the moon intersects its line of the nodes every 18.6 years. Double the 18.6 time period and you arrive at 37.2. Much more work needs to be done with stock market cycles, but the basic periods of importance (well identified in my stock market book) fit hand-in-glove with the moon's wobbles.

Sociologists and criminologists are perplexed by the fact that crime seems to run in spurts with more crimes being reported during full moons. Of course, we are all familiar with the term "lunatic", but not too many people realize that the word derives from "lunar" — moon.

What I'm trying to demonstrate is that the moon does, most definitely, exert strong influences on human behavior. That influence is so strong, I contend, as to directly influence a number of commodities. Exactly how this comes about, I do not know. But I do know that I have repeatedly watched several commodities respond with precise accuracy to new moon "sell signals" and full moon "buy signals".

## MY BEST LINE

At one time, when I was giving numerous stock market seminars around the country, I was always assured of reviving the interest of my audience when I began talking about the moon. The astrology buffs would see me as a convert to their cause while the professional skeptics were perplexed and vexed about the high degree of correlation between the moon and prices.

I would repeatedly emphasize that I am not an astrologer (I know precious little about the subject). I am a speculator, an observer. When I observe something that appears to be causative, my speculative antenna pop up. I must investigate that phenomena whether it's the moon, bio-rhythms, chart formations or money supply figures. The true speculator is, at heart, a researcher in pursuit of the unanswerable. Thus, while most find the moon theory a bit "too much" for them, I have found it an interesting and rewarding area of study.

## THE BUY SIGNAL

A buy signal is forecast for Silver, Wheat, Corn and Soy Bean Oil whenever a full moon appears. The occurance of a full moon may spot the exact day of a low or a rally, or it may be one day early or late. This is immaterial to me. What does matter is that on, or about the time of the full moon period, these prices usually rally. This gives me ample time to begin thinking about what I want to buy and then refine my exact purchases.

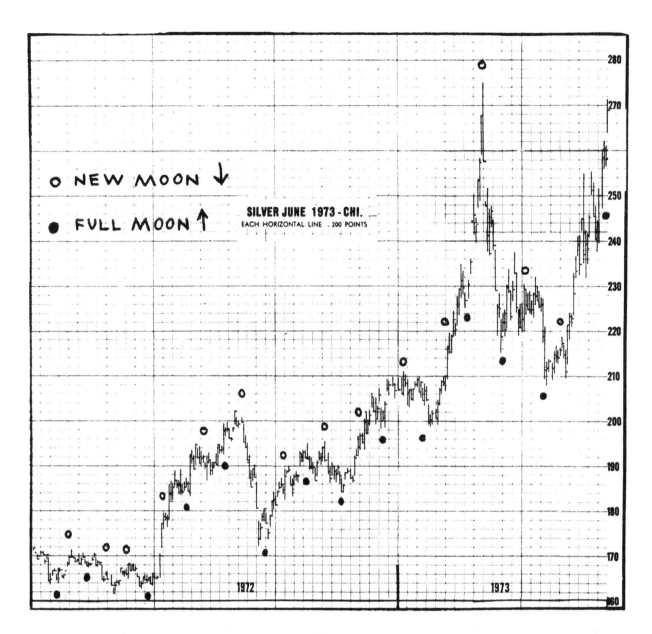

O NEW MOON ↓

● FULL MOON ↑

SILVER JUNE 1973 - CHI.
EACH HORIZONTAL LINE · 200 POINTS

## THE SELL SIGNALS

A sell signal for the above mentioned commodities is given when the moon "disappears", or becomes a new moon. As the moon appears to contract to nothingness, mankind draws the purse strings and down go prices.

Interestingly, the new moon plunges to a temperature of -260° at this time. In a bull market the new moon signals small pull backs while the full moon spots the great buying times. It's reversed for bear markets.

On the long term silver chart shown here, I've shown the times a full moon appeared. These are marked by a filled in circle just below the prices. The appearance of a new moon is indicated by the circle above prices. As you can see, in total there are 28 buy and sell signals from the moon.

94

Out of 18 occurances, some 15 correctly forecast future prices. I submit for your judgment ... is this not superior to most of the technical indicators you are currently using?

The chart on Soy Bean Oil presents some fascinating figures for we moon watchers. There are sixteen new and full moons. Only two moon signals would not have been profitable. Certainly such a high degree of reliability exceeds that expected from chance alone. Perhaps this is a controlling influence in our lives.

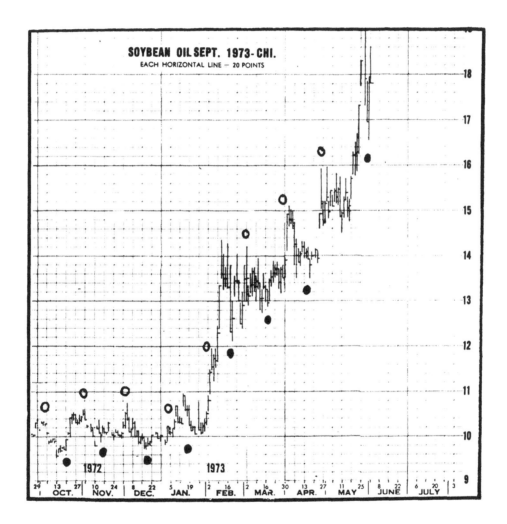

Next, look at the Corn chart. There are twenty-two moon signals. Of the twenty-two there are really no bad signals. The astute trader was forewarned of every turn because he knew the moon's reversal pattern was in process.

To be sure, we cannot follow anything blindly, not even the moon (no pun intended). But, we should pay close attention to these vital phases and be ready to act accordingly, in phase with this master cycle.

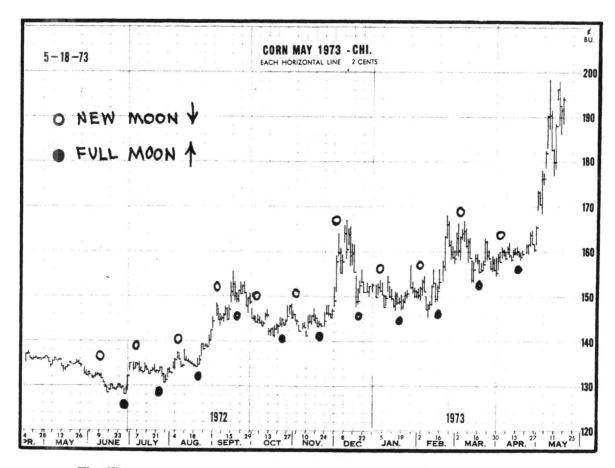

5-18-73

CORN MAY 1973 - CHI.
EACH HORIZONTAL LINE    2 CENTS

○ NEW MOON ↓

● FULL MOON ↑

1972          1973

The Wheat chart also presents some pretty convincing proof there is definitely something "out there" fooling around with our commodity prices. Notice the number of times the full moon was right on the button, or very close to calling bottoms particularly in the 1973 Wheat bull market. Also observe how profitable it would have been to sell on the new moon signals.

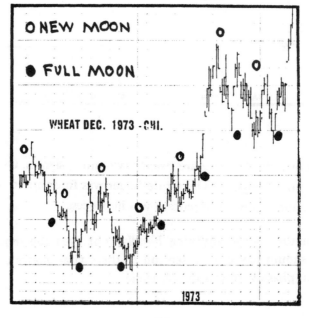

○ NEW MOON

● FULL MOON

WHEAT DEC. 1973 - CHI.

1973

96

I am so thoroughly convinced of the moon's influence, that I use close stops, and/or sell if prices fail to rally during the start of a new moon — that is, when prices are weak in the midst of what should be a bullish phase. Any market that can't get moving when these strong influences are being exerted is not a very healthy market.

The slide rule set will whip out their slip sticks to work out the Chi-squared test to determine the reliability of moon signals. Others will argue that this was just a coincidence of the 1973 market.

Perhaps. But, when you consider new moon tendencies have been analyzed and contemplated since the turn of the century; that the theory has been expounded upon and written about by many others, you will have to admit (perhaps with reluctance) that it may have indeed been more than a coincidence as far as the 1973 market was concerned.


## THE SUGAR SECRET

My good friend, Mort Cleveland, with Commodity Closeup, uses the moon a great deal. While I was the first one, to my knowledge, to talk about Silver and the moon, (Pugh only wrote about grains and the moon) Cleveland has used the positions of the moon to time commodity trades. You should see a copy of his letter for full details on all commodities.

One of Cleveland's little known tricks is this gem; sugar tends to decline when the moon is at its greatest declination South — and rallies when the moon is at its greatest declination North. Incidentally, these terms and time periods are found in any of the popular Farmers' Almanacs that cost about $.50 a copy.


The Sugar charts shown here give a good indication of the reliability of sugar to respond to lunar activity. The time period from the declination is thirteen days. Thus, Sugar traders should keep their eyes open for reversals in the Sugar market in cadence with this thirteen day time period.

Cleveland's work also suggests that Cocoa rallies approximately 75% of the time at the start of a new moon. I checked the figures myself (see the Cocoa chart) and found them correct.

Please don't take moon signals as absolutes. They are not. But, they are reliable indications of when we should be on the lookout for reversals. Just because we have a full moon does not mean that Wheat and Silver will rally. But, it's a pretty good bet, in the sense of probabilities, that commodities will rally at that time. Speculators . . . act accordingly.

97

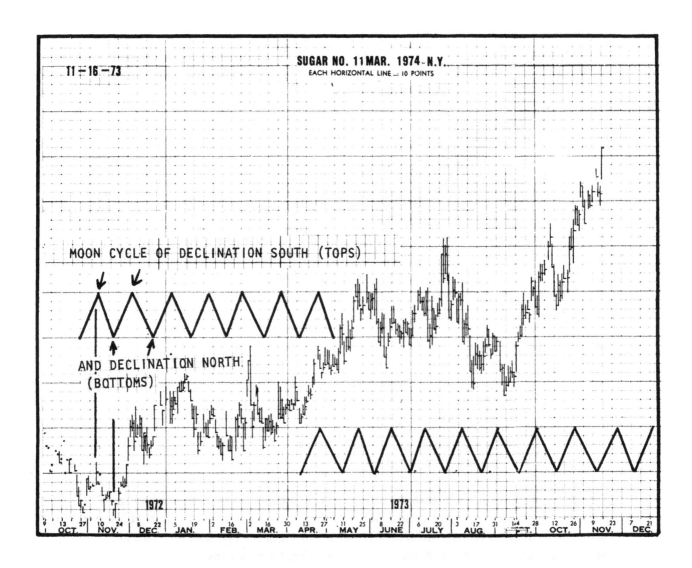

SUGAR NO. 11 MAR. 1974-N.Y.
EACH HORIZONTAL LINE — 10 POINTS

11 - 16 - 73

MOON CYCLE OF DECLINATION SOUTH (TOPS)

AND DECLINATION NORTH
(BOTTOMS)

Research done on the number of births at the full moon and new moon (Methodist Hospital of Southern California) shows that 17% more babies were born, on the average, during the full moon period. This does not mean all babies will be born at the full moon just as a full moon does not mean a Silver rally will start at that time. But, it puts the probabilities substantially in our favor.

When the truth is known, I suspect we will find most cyclical activity is caused by lunar, solar, and planetary influences. That cycles do exist is intriguing. What causes those cycles is even more fascinating.

98

## SPECIAL HINTS ON THE USE OF THIS UNIQUE METHOD

Expect big bull moves to begin at a time of the full moon. See the Silver and Wheat charts.

If, at the next new moon you sell out a long position you took down during the full moon, only to see prices move higher — step right back in because prices will continue trending up to the next full moon. At that time prices will really start to zoom and will enter a blow-off phase.

As a final point for your consideration, I suggest you contemplate the fact the gigantic 1973 Bull market underwent its largest correction during the last week in August. You guessed it . . . right in phase with the new moon! Get to know the moon!

CHAPTER NINE




HOW TRANSACTIONAL ANALYSIS HELPED MAKE MY MILLION DOLLARS

## CHAPTER 9

## HOW TRANSACTIONAL ANALYSIS HELPED MAKE MY MILLION DOLLARS

If you take the time to read stock or commodity research and surveys done at the turn of the century, an interesting statistic keeps popping up. Surveys, at that time, indicated 95% of traders, investors, speculators (call them what you will) lost money. Only 5% beat the market.

Current articles in the Wall Street Journal as well as reports of public hearings and articles in financial magazines indicate a similar fact — 95% of the investors are losers — only 5% winners.

Imagine, despite our ten-fold improvement in market data, market theories, technical and fundamental tools, we still have the same ratio of winners to losers!

This tells me there's a great deal more to beating the market than having the best set of tools. Indeed, beating the market, I reasoned, means getting my head on straight in relation to the markets. Since my first attempt at understanding personal motivation, I've observed a goodly number of winners and losers in this game and feel my comments may be of some value to you. I hope so.

Making money in the market presents a difficult psychological problem to many people for two reasons. The first is our natural reaction to market news. It is invariably wrong. Everyday logic does not work in the market. That's why attorneys and doctors are widely known among broker circles as the biggest "pidgeons". These men have been trained to act according to a logical sequence pattern. Thus, the "well-educated" professionals bomb out along with everyone else.

The second reason we all experience difficulty in beating the market is, I feel, directly related to our own self image and early childhood motivation. I know that at this point I may lose a few readers — the real market losers!

I say that, because invariably, the biggest market losers I've ever known were absolutely paranoid about exposing their thoughts (about themselves) to others.

One fellow, who simply must be put into the category of the biggest all-time losers, managed to get one of my unlisted phone numbers and called for advice. I suggested to him that any market advice I could give him would be of no value unless he was prepared to knowledgeably act upon it. He told me his story; how he lost the funds of his small, profit sharing company and how he could not tell his wife, or the Puerto Rican workers (who were a majority of the investors). I readily perceived that he was a man definitely on the skids.

For one reason or another he had managed to run $250,000 into $20,000 in three short years — good years at that. He did it by always falling for someone's pitch; a hot story or a new technical system. Though he could blame others for leading him astray, he admitted that, in all cases, he made the final decisions.

Now you tell me. Why would a grown man, apparently well educated, continually seek out bad people, bad deals — and then hold on to them far beyond the point of no return!

My personal feeling is that the man wanted to lose money — to show a weakness — in hope of finding true appreciation, love, recognition, (any or all of those deficiencies could be sufficient motivation) from a wife, mother, father or some other strong family influence. In many respects, market losers are like little boys that deliberately misbehave just to attract their mother's attention. For a child, this is not necessarily an unacceptable method for getting parental attention.

For an adult, this behavior pattern is not acceptable.

If you take the time to study any of the popular transactional analysis books such as, Games People Play, I'm OK, You're OK, or Born to Live, I think you'll be impressed with the hypothesis established therein; many of us are spending our lives acting out games or roles. These "games" are oftimes a product of our early childhood experiences.

What about the woman that marrys an alcoholic, only to divorce him and marry another alcoholic. Certainly she's playing a role; "Oh look at me, pity me, aren't I wonderful and generous to give so much of myself to this S.O.B.?"

And what of the habitual criminal? Smart criminals are not caught. The Cosa Nostra has shown us that. Yet, most criminals (who are psychological losers) always manage to leave a fingerprint, a shoelace, or some clue to help identify them. Why? Surely, by the time a man has served two or three terms in prison he must know how to perform a "clean" burglary. But, they never can.

101

So it is with stock market losers. Perhaps, in their childhood their parents told them money was "the cause of all evil." Now that they are well paid executives or successful business men, at times that admonishing voice still persists from the grave. The voice subtly reminds them that money is "bad". It acts as a negative force in their life, especially that "doesn't matter" money which they are taking such wild, speculative chances on.

## COMMODITY WINNERS: WHAT THEY HAVE IN COMMON

Winners in the markets have several things in common. Perhaps the most important trait they share is an expansive mind. Winners are able to transcend shackles that bind them to earlier childhood experiences which negate opportunities for optimum success.

In my case, I have repeatedly caught myself making trades on which I knew I would lose. Yet, for some inexplicable reason, I simply had to go through with it. I did ... and I lost. I realized, quickly enough, that I was not tied down by early edicts. As an individual, I could win in the market and be free.

Winners are not obstinate people. We are quick to admit our errors and nothing, absolutely nothing in the market is real to us in the sense that it has a "value."

Losers, on the other hand, are very stubborn people who refuse to accept facts, losses and their own poor judgment.

When a winner and a loser buy Pork Bellies at the same time, for the same price, only to see it decline, one sees an interesting contrast of philosophies. The loser immediately tries to justify his error. He'll court the opinion of others, urging them to support his view. He holds onto his position, arguing the rest of the world is wrong and he's right.

The winner, on the other hand, is quick to take his loss. He doesn't care whether he's right or wrong; that's not the name of the game. The game is making money, not whether he's right or wrong. He knows too, that he may be wrong many, many times and right only once — but he'll still walk away a very big winner.

The winner has no illusions about his intellect. Thus, he readily admits errors. The winner has supreme self confidence. He probably inflates himself, telling himself that he is good, that he is invincible, that he can master the market. He may do this openly or subconsciously, and so often that it becomes an integral part of his personality. He knows, beyond a shadow of a doubt, that he can beat the hell out of the market.

## IDENTIFYING A FEW MARKET "GAMES"

### THE "DUMB BROKER" GAME

This is one game losers love to play. While I'm the first to admit that most brokers are not going to help you make money in the market, I must concede that many clients want to lose and use the broker-client relationship to do so. One method of play is to open accounts with a number of brokers so the loser can always blame at least one of them for his errors.

Again, the broker becomes the "whipping boy" for not using stops, for not selling out, for not telling about a "vital" piece of news, or for obscuring the dangers of this game. To a certain extent the blame is validly placed as you'll see in a moment. But let's keep in mind that we are adults; traders should not be relying on their brokers for information. This is indicative of emotional weakness, the search for the father figure to help us out of our current problem.

### THE "DUMB CLIENT" GAME

If the truth were to be known, you'd find that at least 60% of commodity brokers lost all their money trading futures and can only support their habit by becoming brokers.

This group of losers, who have thoroughly infiltrated the brokerage houses in recent years, will do everything possible to shoot down a market winner. They'll call with too much information, mislead and make him nervous by overstating situations. These brokers abhor a winner and will do their utmost to obviate their client's success.

### THE "HELP ME — I'M JUST A POOR COUNTRY BOY" GAME

This is the game that keeps mutual funds and advisory services in business. Both winners and losers keep the game alive. Winners play by realizing they don't know a blessed thing about the market so they seek out winners to handle their funds . . . to help them.

Losers play the game either by seeking out another loser to manage or advise them, or by spotting a winner from whom they beg and plead help. What they're really after is a bit of advice so they can "do it themselves". They are not prepared to let a winner call the shots. They must show the world how smart they are and do it on their own.

## THE "LET ME REST" GAME

Another common market game is played by the harried executive or business man who has burned himself out getting to the top. He's "made it", but the pressures are ungodly. He won't admit to himself that he desperately wants to get off the treadmill. How can he do it? One way is by losing money . . . all his money . . . to the point of bankruptcy which means he can return to more humble days with less pressure. So, he becomes a loser.

## WHY I LIKE LOSERS

I love market losers because they are the people who give me hundreds of thousands of dollars each year. After all, the money I made in 1973, the million plus dollars, had to come from someone and I don't think it came from the commercials. It came from people that wanted to lose it. Perhaps they could not afford the loss, but lose it they did.

## HOW TO BECOME A WINNER

If your brokerage account indicates that you are a loser, or you've experienced a few twinges reading this chapter, you need help in becoming a winner. Here's how to do it.

First, try to develop some psychological insight. Read some of the transactional analysis books mentioned earlier. Don't be ashamed to try a bit of self-identification and analysis.

There was a certain gentleman — well known as a genius in the commodity market for his ability to spot big market moves — who never made any money at the game. This seems rather unbelievable until one considers the psychological motivation that prevented him from putting his money where and when it would bring him vast profits. After a brief venture into transactional analysis, this gentleman was able to discover some rather surprising facets to his psychological makeup. He was able to identify the causes of his failures and thereby remedy the situation. He is now a two-way winner; he makes the calls and collects the cash.

Reading books of this nature will provide you with the insight to which I refer. That's the path I took. I began to understand the reasons for my unprofitable actions. My next step was to consciously tell myself that I could and would be a winner. I had succeeded in everything else I had undertaken and the market was not to be an exception. I would beat the market by learning more about myself, my motives, my conditioning; and would do it through self-discipline.

104

My approach involves a good deal of meditation, prayer and self evaluation. It is a matter of concentrating on beating the market; a matter of letting myself know that even during the worst possible times I can recover by maintaining my self balance and by adhering to my well-defined game plan.

I am a winner! I will win in the market!

You can too, merely by a slight change of emphasis. Rather than dwelling on how difficult the market is, think of how much money you can make. Every negative vibration has the unique ability to nullify two positive vibrations. It must become an integral part of your personality to see yourself a winner.

This means visualizing your profits and planning for the good that can be derived from these profits. After all, money, by itself, is nothing. You must do something with the money once the necessities have been taken care of. Be altruistic. Put your money in places where others may benefit from it, but always think "success".

Perhaps just the sight of your broker's puzzled face, as you make one profitable trade after another, will be enough motivation!

The meditation, or prayer method may not be entirely palatable to many readers. To me, prayer or meditation are both similar levels of conscious receptivity. At these levels, the mind seems to open up its power sources to the demands you wish to make.

I do it by relaxing. Ideally, for me, it is done out of doors, in a beautiful, God-inspired setting. I try to completely empty my mind of thoughts. It is not easy to arrive at this stage, but when you do, you can begin to re-program yourself.

Keep this up for several minutes; much longer is fatiguing. I sincerely believe there is nothing in life that is unattainable . . . if you really want it! Making a fortune in the market is merely a matter of wanting it badly enough to give up your fishing, golf, or other pastimes near and dear to your heart in order to focus attentions and concentrate energies on the market.

You must talk with yourself . . . openly discussing what is preventing you from making more money. Are you failing to use stops; not concentrating on the big moves, or overtrading? Identify the cause, then tell your subconscious, the Alpha wave level, that you are no longer going to commit those errors. As Emeile Cove taught her followers to say, "Every day, in every way, I'm getting better and better".

105

CHAPTER TEN

MY  PRICELESS TRADING HINTS

# CHAPTER 10

## MY PRICELESS TRADING HINTS

Readers of my first book, "The Secret of Selecting Stocks for Immediate and Substantial Gains", have told me one of their favorite chapters was the one giving my priceless stock market trading hints. Therefore, I decided to do the same in this book. Do not confuse my stock market trading hints with the following commodity insights. They are, at times, radically different.

Hopefully, after reading this chapter, you will acquire an immediate, in depth feeling for the market's diverse tactics. Yes, diverse tactics! After many years of watching prices bounce around, I'm convinced the market does not want us to get the best executions and thereby, deliberately leads us astray. Here's how to avoid some of the "traps" that occur every day.

### HOW TO PROFIT FROM THE MORNING BULGE

A price bulge occurs when there is an over-supply of buyers or sellers. It may be a downside bulge, (price break) or an upside movement. My studies suggest that 70% of the time, there is a commodity price bulge during the first hour of trading. This is even truer if the previous day's action has been very strong or very weak.

Last week, Pork Bellies had two limit up days. The second day saw prices closing at their highs. The stage was set for a price bulge because there was suddenly an imbalance of buyers. Prices bulged the next morning as they opened up the limit. People that bought were immediately proven wrong because prices dropped almost 200 points. Many were stopped out, only to see prices recover later in the day, closing back up to the limit.

My price bulge theory says that we should never buy strength during the first hour of market activity, especially following a strong close on the previous day.

This is not to say that buying should never be done during the first hour of trading. I merely stress that in the event of a bulge, (showing a large move in the first hour) it's best to step to the sidelines and wait for a minor correction during the day.

106

## HOW TO SPOT COMMODITY CYCLES

It seems as though everything man has deduced about his activities can be broken down into cyclical activity. There is a cycle to international wars (this one peaks in 1984), to traffic deaths in New York City and even to a well-defined cycle of Negro lynchings in the South! So, it's certainly no surprise to find that most commodities have rythmic vibrations that evolve into cyclical behavior.

Should cycles fascinate you, you can subscribe to services that use computers to break down the various cyclical components. Such services cost about $300 per year.

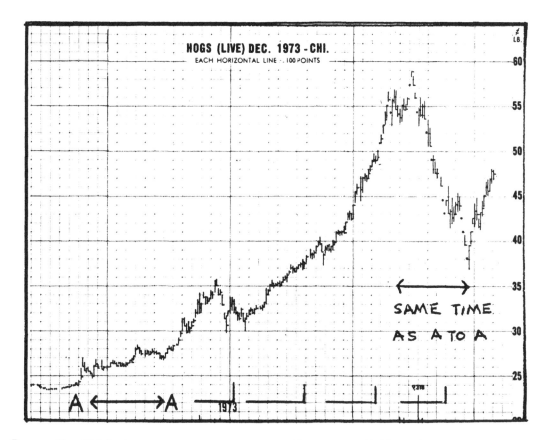

Personally, I'd just as soon save my money. I can get reliable indications of an important cycle by counting the number of days between each important low seen on the chart for any given commodity. Let's take Pork Bellies as an example. According to the chart on page 66, Pork Bellies have been making some sort of bottom attempt about every 25 days.

If we can locate the last few significant bottoms, all we need do is count forward, the length of this cycle, to arrive at an estimation of where the next cycle should begin. Simple, isn't it? Amazingly enough, this method will very closely forecast, in advance, when you should begin positioning for the next move.

107

Selling points are arrived at in the same manner. Simply take the number of days from one top to the next and count out this distance from the most recent top. During that time period some selling should enter the market, and perhaps a top will be made.

While cycles are very helpful in selecting the general time period in which to look for buys or sells, they cannot forecast the magnitude of the coming move. This is strictly a timing tool. It does not portend how large the move will be. In a strong bear market the buying periods indicated by the cycles will show small rallies or trading ranges before the dominant bearish forces are again exerted.

Notice on the chart for December Hogs how well timed the cycle measurement (marked A to A) is in forecasting the following market rallies. Also, notice that it does not forecast the extent of the moves — just when they should come.


## WHEN TO BUY AT THE OPENING

I have found that opening orders usually give very poor executions. There are only two times when you should buy at the opening.

The best time to use an opening order is when you want to buy a commodity that you feel is about to stage a good rally. The commodity must be oversold. This means the commodity's per cent reading, discussed earlier, should be below 85%. Secondly, check to see if the commodity closed at, or close to, its low for the day.

If these conditions do exist, it's an almost sure thing prices will get clobbered the following morning — with a bulge — right on the opening where the lows for the day are usually established.

In the event the commodity does not break apart at the seams, giving you a splendid fill on the opening, you will be buying at a very good time. Why? Simply because any time a commodity should go down, as indicated by the previous day's close, (while it's in an oversold area) and it doesn't go down, indicates that it has gone against expectations. Hence, it is very bullish, and you still wind up with a good execution.

Of course, you reverse the process for selling or shorting. You look for an overbought condition. Then you need a day that closes at its high. The following morning, should you be inclined to sell or short, would be the time to use an opening order.

More money goes down the tubes on opening orders than you can imagine. The opening prices in commodities are usually a good distance away from the previous day's close. This gap will almost always be filled during the day if you'll just have the patience to wait for the inevitable pull-back.

## WHEN TO USE MARKET ORDERS

I feel you should use a market order only when you are in a big rush to buy the commodity. When you absolutely must have it. Now, what would force you into "demanding" the future contract?

In my situation, I will use the market order if:

1. I've been trying for several days to get a fill and have failed by bidding under the market. I must get the positions, so I market it.

2. Commodities are in a deep sell off (or a strong rally) which I deduce to be a false move. Should I see prices down the limit, when I suspect they should not, I'll use market orders. It's too hard to say when prices will start to come back. I'm shooting for the low and I don't want to miss it by too wide a margin.

Then, and only then, are market orders justified.

The secret here is in <u>not</u> following the crowd. While everyone wants to sell, you are buying in a situation where you expect an immediate snap-back of prices.

## HOW A VERY SMALL TRADER CAN "TEST" THE MARKET

In the old days, Livermore and Keene were said to have "tested" the market. If the market was bullish, they would sell. That's right — they would sell a few contracts of the commodity. If they found it easy to sell, (and more importantly, the sale showed a quick profit) they knew the market was not strong and they should avoid making their long purchase at that time. As you can well imagine, testing the market requires vast sums of money and just as much courage.

Can the small trader accomplish the same? I think so. In fact, I have repeatedly "tested" the market without risking a single cent. Anyone can do it! It's not done by buying or selling, but by waiting until you are really interested in a market.

At that point, you say to yourself, "OK, I'm going to test the market to see if it's really strong. I'll do this by pretending to sell 100,000 bushels of Wheat," or whatever. Instead of selling, you wait until the ticker tape says that amount of the commodity has been sold.

109

Then sit back, see how well the market absorbs the selling. If the market shrugs its shoulder and moves higher you know the market is strong. Now you can buy.

Talk about free-riding! This is the greatest way in the world to let other people's money show you how bullish or bearish the market really is. Let some other poor devil worry about the 100,000 bushels of Wheat he's just shorted or sold. That's his problem. But, his selling will give you a tremendous insight to the market — free of charge!

If you do not have access to a ticker tape, simply wait a few hours after you decide to buy. If prices are still strong your chances of buying a winner are greatly improved.

## THE SECRET OF THREE

I can't tell you why, but it appears whenever I try to get a commodity and miss on my first two entry points, by raising a third time I do get the commodity, and a loss, because prices quickly reverse themselves.

Yes, it's true. Whenever we become so urgent in our demands for a commodity, especially if it's rallying, we invariably buy right at the top. The trick here is to keep your "cool" and avoid chasing prices.

The first one and a half hours of trading each day can be broken up into three, one half hour segments. Purchases made in the third half hour (if prices have been up) are not as likely to be correct as those made in the first segment. This is, of course, reversed for bear trends.

You'll also find the third day of a rally usually makes a short term top. Any time prices have moved up, three days in a row, the odds are 82% for a down move on the fourth and fifth day.

## THE FIVE DAY MAJOR MOVE SIGNAL

This is an interesting technical signal that works quite well. It's rather simple and has certainly spotted some great moves. The signal is given when prices close, up, five days in a row. Such a display of unusual strength means a further up move is ahead. In the case of a bear market, prices down five days in a row mean you can expect lower prices.

This does not mean the major move will continue on the sixth day. It does indicate that after five days you had better be looking for a spot in which to take a position.

110

Any time prices have been in a trading range, and suddenly move in the same direction five days in a row without interruption, you know there is plenty of pent up demand in that market. Be prepared for a great deal more action!

## WHAT ARE THE ODDS FOR AN ADVANCE THIS MONTH?

Most commodities have strong seasonal tendencies. I'll discuss this in a moment, but for now, let's turn our attention to an advisory service, Commodity Futures Statistics Service, published by Len Kuker.

In each week's market letter, Kuker gives subscribers a table showing the percentage of times that each commodity has risen in price the following month during the past ten years. Mr. Kuker's research shows that during the last ten years, December Wheat has risen 90% of the time in October, while December Corn has risen only 10% during the month of October.

January Platinum, according to Len, has risen 100% during the month of September within the last ten years. March Sugar has risen only 20% of the time and so on, for the twenty most actively traded commodities.

Certainly, no one would buy a commodity just because of the seasonal tendency, but it's a nice, confirming tool, enabling us to see the price bias in your favor. It's also a good tool for calling attention to a certain commodity you might otherwise overlook.

You can get a sample copy of Kuker's letter by writing to him at Box 682, Somerville, NJ 08876.

There are some other pretty reliable seasonal tendencies of which you should be aware. Orange Juice, one of the better indications, invariably starts a strong rally during the first two weeks of October. Please notice the long term charts. You can see how all the truly large juice rallies have begun at that approximate time.

You'll also find that Pork Bellies usually have large up moves that begin in August and the last week in October. Wheat is usually a good buy about June 1st, October 1st, and on December 1st. Potatoes have a seasonal tendency to begin rallying on September 1st and they become a sell just about mid-March of the following year.

Eggs have a nice base from which to rise in late June to the end of December when they are usually a good sale.

Strangely enough, Wheat and Pork Bellies both represent good selling opportunities in May of each year.

111

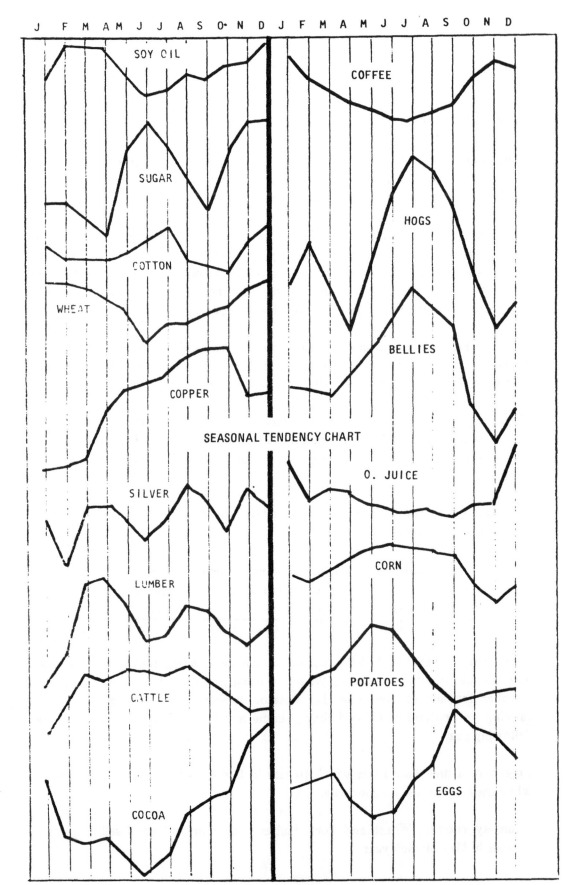

SEASONAL TENDENCY CHART

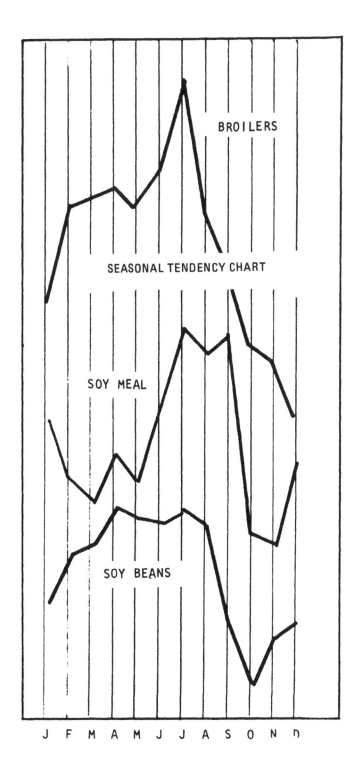

Corn often sets up a buying point in mid-March. Broilers usually get moving to the upside in January of each year and Cocoa sees buying in late July.

The following charts are for your information and study. I've made my notes but there are other seasonal tendencies you should learn for yourself. I suggest you continually monitor these superb charts.

## MORE INFORMATION ON THE COMMERCIALS

If, at this point, you've learned nothing else from this book, you should have developed a great deal of respect for commercial doings in the market as opposed to the workings of the speculators. You've been told about Open Interest, premiums and the large trader report. There is, however, another way to get even more information on the commercials.

This involves using your friendly broker. Have him go to the floor of the exchange and ask who has been doing the buying and the selling.

The answer will come back that it was either the locals, the commercials, or brokerage house activity.

By and large, the locals and the brokerage houses are not particularly astute. Therefore, little is learned when they were the day's greatest motivating force. When and if your broker learns that the commercials, Cargil, Peavey, etc. have been responsible for the action — that's something to be concerned about.

It is even more meaningful if you check the floor each day and see a trend developing, i.e., in persistent commercial buying. This is magnified even more if they have been buying during a time of extended price weakness. If the commercials are willing to step into a falling market, you have uncovered an excellent trading possibility.


## WHERE TO PLACE STOPS

If you trade, you must use stops. The most common method of placing stops revolves around prices breaking through what should have been a support area. This is certainly nothing new. If prices fall below yesterday's low, or the lowest low of the last four days, many "systems" would stop you out.

My method uses stops in two ways. One is based on price, the other on time.

When carefully studying your chart, searching for a stop point, you must realize that others are doing the same thing. The rest of the traders will usually place stops slightly below the supposed support area. In this example, most traders would have placed their stops at, or slightly below the low point marked at A on the chart.

Realizing this, I place my stop order just a little bit lower than where I suspect other people have placed theirs. In this case, my stop would be at B. I am thereby assured. "If they are going to get me, they're going to have to take a lot of other people along first."

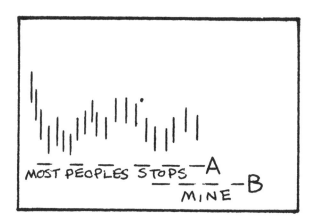

A second price method is ideal for the system trader or beginner. This method dictates that you will not take more than a $400 loss on any one contract trade. That amount becomes your fixed stop point. Basically, this is the way we use stops in our advisory service. We are seldom willing to expose subscribers to a loss greater than $400.

Such a plan is clean and simple. All you need do is tell your broker where to place the stop in terms of dollars risk. For the novice, or the person who lacks discipline, this is the very best possible system.

## TIME STOPS

You can also stop yourself out of a commodity by demanding it perform within a certain time period. If it does not, you get out of it, automatically. Let's say you buy Wheat on Monday. If the move for which you are looking has not begun by Thursday, I would suggest you get out. This means you are using a four day stop. The commodity must start the projected move in four days or there is an indication that something is not right and you'll have to move back to the sidelines. After carefully studying thousands of charts and making thousands of trades, I have come to the conclusion the four day time period is the optimum span to use for time stops. Waiting any longer can get you in serious trouble. Not allowing that much time will get you out too soon.

## HOW TO USE MENTAL STOPS

Many traders say they use mental stops. This means, when a trader concludes a price has fallen to a level they consider risky, they begin selling.

Here, the advantage lies in the fact your stop is known only to you, not floor brokers. In theory, this sounds fine. However, I do not know of anyone that has successfully used mental stops. As prices smash down to the mental selling level, we begin to re-evaluate and, in the process, fail to use the mental stop. Here's an example:

A few years ago, a widely followed advisory service recommended a stock giving an actual stop point in the letter. The advisor also bought the stock for his clients but selected a mental stop.

As luck would have it, the stock broke badly, hitting the stops announced in the market letter and giving the subscribers a four to six point loss. However, the advisor did not use the mental stop for his managed accounts hoping for a comeback so he could sell. Unfortunately, in this case, the stock never did come back. Instead, it plummeted to zero, wiping out the advisor and his clients who had relied on the mental stop.

## A FINAL COMMENT ON OPEN INTEREST

The alert trader will constantly monitor Open Interest figures to help him time some of his trades. The signal to buy occurs when Open Interest drops greatly in one or two days while, at the same time, our other indices are telling us a buy signal is in sight.

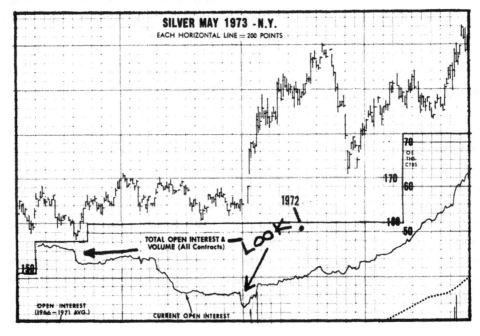

Should you doubt the significance of one or two day Open Interest reductions, I'd suggest you study the Silver chart shown here. Notice how some of the biggest rallies in Silver started right after a huge, one day decline in Open Interest.

116

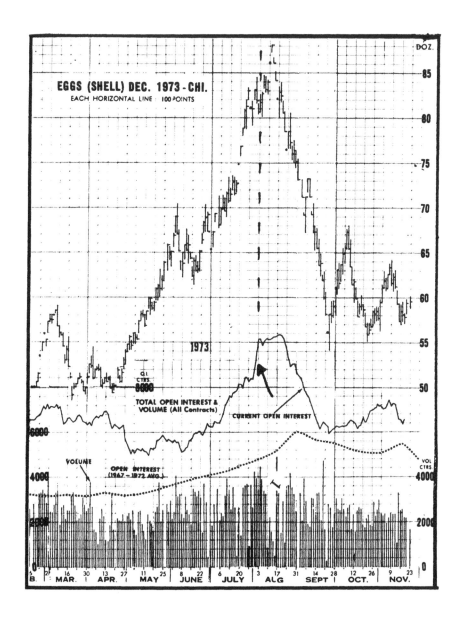

Also, notice December Eggs and the major top they made in August of 1972. Observe the tremendous advance in Open Interest on one day shortly before the all time high.

In March 1973 Flax gave a nice Open Interest buy signal as the Open Interest smashed down some 10% in two days. The important thing is the Open Interest reduction be very quick and large. Such a change is a reliable indication that the market has undergone a radical re-evaluation by the commercials and a trend change is in the making.

You'll also find that Open Interest divergence from the season's tendencies are also significant. There are several ways to look at this.

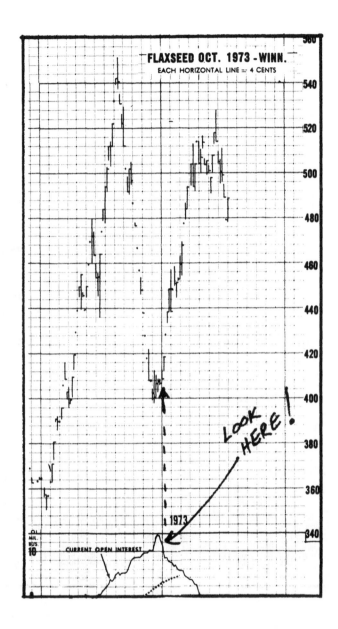

If Open Interest declines more than the seasonal tendency, or more than the three year average as shown in the Commodity Research Bureau Charts Service, you may well be onto a buy. Or, Open Interest may be declining at a time when the seasonal pattern indicates a rise. This also sets up a buy.

Notice how the booming Belly market of 1973 saw both such happenings. The Open Interest was very bullish, forecasting higher prices. It was much lower than the seasonal tendency, and often failed to move up when an increase was the seasonal tendency.

Such deviations from the norm provide valuable insight to markets.

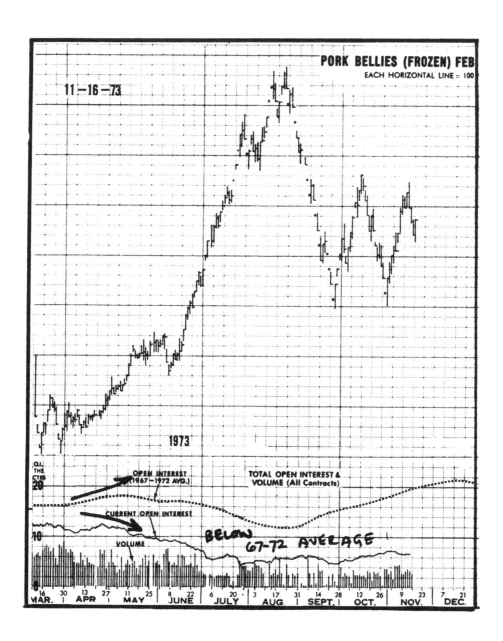

11—16—73

1973

CL.
THS.
CTRS.
20

OPEN INTEREST
(1967—1972 AVG.)

TOTAL OPEN INTEREST &
VOLUME (All Contracts)

CURRENT OPEN INTEREST

BELOW 67-72 AVERAGE

10

VOLUME

16   30   13   27   11   25   8   22   6   20   3   17   31   14   28   12   26   9   23   7   21
MAR.  |  APR.  |  MAY  |  JUNE  |  JULY  |  AUG.  |  SEPT. |  OCT.  |  NOV.  |  DEC.

## HOW TO FORECAST TOMORROW'S HIGH AND LOW

While I'll readily admit it is not possible to always predict the exact high and low of tomorrow's market, today, I do want to introduce a forecasting formula that will consistently indicate about where the next day's price will go.

## MY PIVOT PRICE FORMULA

To arrive at tomorrow's probable high add today's high, low and close. Divide this number by three. For reference, I'll call this the Pivot Price. Subtract the Pivot Price from yesterday's low. Then add this difference back onto the pivot price and you will have a projection of tomorrow's high.

119

Here's an example: On October 24, 1973, March sugar had a high of 9.60, a low of 9.22, and a close of 9.55. Add these three figures together and you arrive at 2837, divide this by three to arrive at the pivot price of 9.45. Next subtract the low, 9.22, from the pivot price of 9.45. The forecast move is .23 which you add to the pivot price, 9.45 + 23 = 9.68 is forecast as the next day's high.

On October 25, 1973, March sugar made a daily high price at 9.70!

To forecast tomorrow's low, today, arrive at the pivot price, then subtract the pivot price from today's high. Then, subtract this difference from the pivot price and you have established where tomorrow's low should be, assuming tomorrow will be a down day.

Here's an illustration of forecasting tomorrow's low. On October 24, 1973, March Cocoa had a range of 57.29, 55.25, and close of 56.25. Add these numbers together, then divide by three and you arrive at a pivot price of 56.26. Subtract this from the high of 57.29 and the forecast swing is 1.03 subtracted from the pivot price. This predicts that tomorrow's price, if it declines, will be approximately 55.23. The next day March Cocoa made its low at 55.40, a mere .17 points from our forecast point.

In all fairness, I should add that the projected high and low prices are best to use along this manner; if you expect tomorrow to be an up day, then run the formula for the high. That's the one most apt to be correct. By the same token, the low forecast will most likely be correct only if the commodity declines from the next day.

At times, you will find the next day's prices overshooting the projection. When this happens, prices usually go to another level which is the difference between the pivot price and today's total range. As an example, if the pivot price is 65.00, and yesterday's range was 1.50, say 66.50 high and 65.00 low, deduct 1.50 from the pivot price to establish the next low. Add the 1.50 range to the pivot price to project the next high point.

The pivot price formula will not always be correct — do not put too much faith, or time into it. But, I believe it will aid you in selecting stop points, execution levels, etc.

## HOW TO IDENTIFY THE EXACT HIGH OR LOW OF A MOVE

I believe it is possible to repeatedly determine the exact high or low of a short term move. It's so simple that most chartists overlook this important tool. I hope you don't!

120

In my stock market book, I placed great emphasis on the importance of using opening prices in construction of accumulation and distribution patterns in daily volume. Indeed, as far as I'm concerned, that's the secret to stock selection and timing.

In commodities, the opening price level can also be of great importance in detecting reversal days.

Essentially, a reversal day from a down trend to an uptrend develops when prices open lower than the previous day, then go substantially below yesterday's low. Following that, prices recover to close at the top of the daily trading range.

A simple example would be if yesterday's trading range low was 45.00, and today's market opens at 46, then drops to 42.00, rallies to make a high at 47, and closes at 46. This would be an indication that the down trend was through, and an uptrend was about to begin.

An uptrend is all through when prices open high, move higher, and then close at or close to the lows of the day. The illustrations here should give you a pretty good idea of what I'm talking about.

As with any trading tool, it is important to keep in mind that the sell signals will work in established down trends, the buy signals in established uptrends. A sell signal in a bull market has little significance, unless we have seen climatic action and an extended price move of 5-6 months duration.

## THE ULTIMATE TRADING TIP

Developing trading tips is a matter of market experience and observation. I suggest you continually check and cross check the markets to observe what is happening. Take notes. Compare and seek out relationships.

I'm certain you can find a good many other insights to the market. It is done by carefully watching market action and recording your observations so you can come back at a later date and prove out your hunch.

# CHAPTER ELEVEN

## HOW TO START MAKING MONEY TOMORROW MORNING

HOW TO START MAKING MONEY TOMORROW MORNING

Of all the possible investments, I can think of no others offering more appeal for quick, relatively easy money than commodities. I've invested in large real estate projects, commercial paper, banker acceptances, raw land, stocks, bonds; just about everything. But none have been better than commodities. What's more, I believe this good trend is going to continue.

With commodity volume outpacing stock market volume, I'm convinced we are on the verge of a speculative revolution away from securities and into futures. There are many reasons for this. Perhaps foremost is that commodities are easier to trade. Then, there are low margins, and finally, the absolute: commodities are real — stock certificates are fictitious.

Stock market fans talk about the speculative nature of commodities as though the futures markets were some wild and wooly game abounding with tremendous risk. While I'll be the first to admit that commodities do offer risk, I'd like to point out that year after year, several big name companies go, in value, from $50 per share or more to nothing. That's right, the continual stock fiascos such as Penn Central, Revenue Properties, Cameo Records, Equity Funding and Ecological Sciences (to name but a few) are proof positive that stocks are far more risky than commodities.

Corn and Wheat will always have some value. Stocks, on the other hand, can be de-listed, an overnight drop in value to nothing!

As more people see the light the markets will become bigger and more liquid. This will be good, but the commodity markets should not go under the strange metamorphisis that has transformed Wall street. This steadiness in the commodity market will be due to the realistic nature of commodities and the more far-thinking regulatory powers of the CEA vs the SEC. Be that as it may, there's a great future for commodities and at this time, the early 1970's, you are on the ground floor holding the fuse for a real explosion.

Two things will cause this explosion. One is investor disenchantment with the stock market, and two, the tremendous drain we've seen on America's agricultural resources.

Just as in the early 50's, when corporate growth was easy and in demand, we'll now find commodities scarce, and in demand.

122

For years the U.S. government has stored billions of bushels of Wheat, Corn and Soy Beans. We've also warehoused Butter, Eggs and Meat as well as a wide variety of other commodity products. However, that situation no longer exists. According to all government authorities, this country is no longer in the commodity business. Such statements are given in a way that seem to make this situation appear fortuitous.

I suppose it is — for the far-thinking speculator. Remember what happened a few years ago when Americans woke up to the realization that our Gold supply was, for all practical purposes, reduced to zero?

Boom! Up shot the price of gold, from $30.00 an ounce to $120.00.

Prior to this dramatic affair, the Federal Reserve System sent speakers all over the country to convince us that we had enough gold and the price would stabilize in the $30-$40 area. In fact, one such Federal "dog-and-pony show" I witnessed actually suggested the price of gold might drop to $25.

I believe the story will be the same with commodities. This country has lost control of another important economic tool. We purposely stockpiled commodities so the government could smooth out the busts and booms that are part of any dealings with nature's vagaries.

Now, that's all a dream of the past. A good case is the current picture. Government analysts are forecasting record crops for 1974-75. Such crops should be large enough to drive prices down.

We may very well get the record crops. Let's hope so. However, lack of rain, hailstorms, severe drought, blight, or one of a hundred other variables can totally eliminate the hopes for lower prices that result from increased production. Anything goes when it comes to crop shortages. It will be an interesting observation.

That's the key to the next ten years of market action. Assuming the U.S. no longer stock piles; can farmers keep up with the demand and build surpluses to smooth things over during years of agricultural famine?

Enough of my hypothesizing. Let's get back to reality.


## WHAT TO DO TODAY

Assuming you thoroughly understand this book and are ready to begin trading, your first step should be a subscription to an advisory service, some good chart paper and a note book.

Then, armed with your notebook and pen, head for the closest library to get figures on the commodities ,you wish to follow. Check out The Wall Street Journal or The Journal of Commerce.

Make seven columns headed, OPEN — HIGH — LOW — CLOSE — OPEN INTEREST — a column for %R and a final column for the Ten Week Moving Average. Your work sheet will look like this:


OPEN  HIGH  LOW  CLOSE  OPEN INTEREST  %R  10 WK. M.A.


After you have acquired sufficient data about the commodities you want to follow, fifty days should be sufficient time in which to get started, begin running the numbers for indicators. In the event you are lazy, you could write to Commodity Timing, 850 Munras #2, Monterey, California 93940, and we will give you a computer printout with the indicators already constructed as well as all the other necessary data including the difference between the daily close and a twenty day moving average as shown in the sample printout below.


```
                 COMMODITY ?OIL
                 CONTRACT ?7509

DATE      OPEN     HIGH      LOW     CLOSE  CUM OI       50L   25/MOM   %R
750626   21.60    22.15    21.40    21.80   30032      21.21   -0.05    12
750627   22.10    22.20    20.80    20.85   30075      21.13   -1.10    48
750630   20.55    20.80    20.35    20.57   30120      21.05   -1.18    60
750701   20.60    20.70    19.80    19.87   29652      20.97   -0.88    86
750702   19.90    20.35    19.85    20.25   29340      20.91   -0.15    75
750703   20.75    21.25    20.60    21.25   29177      20.87    0.57    40
750707   21.25    21.75    20.90    21.00   28984      20.83    0.50    50
750708   21.05    22.00    21.00    22.00   28655      20.82    2.35     8
750709   22.25    22.95    21.95    22.65   28862      20.83    2.73    10
750710   22.35    23.65    22.35    23.35   29101      20.85    3.30     8
750711   23.40    24.35    23.35    24.35   29514      20.89    4.50     0
750714   24.40    25.25    23.70    23.78   28957      20.92    4.45    27
750715   23.65    24.20    23.25    23.58   28549      20.96    3.66    31
750716   24.00    24.35    23.35    24.25   28765      21.02    4.70    19
750717   24.60    24.60    23.50    23.75   29038      21.08    3.95    38
750718   23.50    23.60    22.80    23.10   29249      21.12    3.90    49
```


The cost of this service is $10.00 for the first fifty days of data for one contract, i.e., December Wheat or March Wheat or May Wheat, etc. This does not include a printout on the entire complex, and $1.50 for each additional ten days you request. This is a great way to save time in calculating back data.

Now that you have your technical information, it's time to plot your charts. Use a nice, crisp-looking paper. Ideally, the scale will be in tenths since that's the unit in which most commodities are traded. You'll quickly have all the historical data laid out in front of you for observation.

A close study of the Commodity Research Bureau Charts, and the daily quote lists in The Journal of Commerce will enable you to select the most promising markets. Study the premiums and the Open Interest pattern. You should also look for seasonal tendencies.

## WHERE MOST OF YOUR TIME SHOULD BE SPENT

Selecting the one or two super trades should consume most of your time. There's a great deal of work and thinking to be done in comparing markets, finding the best Open Interest play and carefully reviewing the premiums. The average tendency is to rush over this section of trading simply because it seems more productive to look at all the technical wiggle-waggles.

In actuality, as I've said so many times, unless you are fundamentally right in your initial selection decisions, all the technical tools will do is get you in trouble. Please devote all your concentration and energies to the selection of your commodities before you give the technical data any consideration at all. Technical data is secondary to screening out the potential big winning trades.

The only technical tool to look at during this screening is the ten week moving average trend line. For a bullish situation it should be slanting up; for a bearish market, it should be slanting down.

## ADDITIONAL HINTS ON USING TECHNICAL TOOLS

At this point, I can assume that you have diligently searched for the most intriguing prospects in the commodity market. If you are like me (and I suspect you are) you will be chomping at the bit to buy or sell the commodities you have selected. That's usually the wrong thing to do.

Countless times I have thoroughly researched my markets, selected the right commodity and had a pretty good feel for where it would go and then lost money on it. Why?

In retrospect, I discovered I had become so worked up and excited about the prospects of the situation that I rushed in. By becoming trigger happy I had purchased far too early, was stopped out, and lost money.

To avoid a similar problem in your trading, I want to encourage you to use the utmost patience in timing your transactions. Await the %R index to give a valid signal or the momentum index to make a long term, trend line penetration. If neither of these developments have occured — be careful.

The chart formation buy and sell signals would be your last resort. They are so very subjective that you'd better make darned certain you understand what I've written about them. Double check to see if the key reversal days have indeed materialized.

We are our own worst enemies. Our lack of patience and inability to wait are the largest single cause for losses. Plus, (as if that's not enough) if indices are close to, or formations look pretty much like that for which we are looking, we rush right in. Don't force the issues. Let the market give you the clear-cut signals I have told you about.

## WHAT TO DO WHEN YOU HAVE YOUR SIGNAL

I am now assuming you have selected the commodity and are right on top of a buy signal. The next question is, how many contracts should you buy — at what time and price — and where should your stop be placed.

As mentioned earlier, you must allocate a fixed amount of money to commodity trading. Whether it is $1,000 or $100,000, you must set aside a certain dollar amount. Gunslingers that end up losers do so because they do not know where they are, financially speaking. Don't let that happen to you.

We are going to beat this game — you and I — by having a set plan of action, and by following it to the letter. Our plan, which I believe unbeatable, says we must know our total dollar amount.

Once we have arrived at that figure I feel it wise to determine how much money you are willing to lose. As a hard and fast rule you should never expose any trade to a loss greater than 5% of your commodity funds (which I'll call equity).

126

Let's say you determine that when prices fall two limit moves you want to get out of the trade. In the case of Pork Bellies, that means $720.00 plus $45.00 in commissions, or $765. If your equity is $10,000 this represents an 8% risk factor for buying just one contract. Accordingly, the mathematics of money management tell us the stop must be moved up so our total loss would be $500.00. Act accordingly. Tell your broker where the stop should be.

At times, you'll see that your stop point can be very close to the market. In that event, you can buy more contracts. Let's say your charts and personal feeling for the markets tell you that you'll want to get out if Bellies decline half a cent. That would be a loss of $180.00 plus commission, per contract.

Using our 5% system of stops means a $10,000 account could buy about three contracts and still be pretty close to our stop rule.

## HOW YOU WILL PROFIT

One of two things will now happen. Prices will move in your favor and you'll have a profit, or, they will move against you and you'll be stopped out.

## WHAT TO DO WHEN YOU ARE STOPPED OUT

Should prices go against you, you will be stopped out. Don't let this get to you. The market does not dislike you and it is not a sign that you have no feel for that particular commodity market. It's merely an indication that you were premature. Do not back away. Remember, you have already identified this as an unusually strong situation.

You should, therefore, move to the sidelines, awaiting another entry point. Do not let the loss befuddle your thinking or bias you against that commodity.

One of my best trades in the fall of 1973 was in the Sugar market. I knew it was going higher, went long, and was stopped out for a loss. The very next day I went right back into the market and bought the same number of contracts I had just been stopped out of. At the time, I was very panicky. Being stopped out on one day and buying back the next can make you look pretty foolish, but that's just what you have to do at times.

You will, of course, want to be studying the markets for other special situations, but don't walk away from the commodity you have already identified as your number one "deal".

127

## HOW PROS HANDLE THEIR PROFITS

The big difference in the method of handling profits (the pros vs the amateurs) is that a pro will not give up any of his gains. Amateurs seem more willing to let loose of their hard earned money.

One of the reasons I was able to do so well in the 1973 market is that I quickly learned not to give up any of my profits. This is accomplished by rapidly exiting bad trades as well as placing liberal stops under your good trades. Traders that made big money at the start of the 1973 Bull market gave almost all of it back because they became careless. They went away on vacations, didn't use stops, or simply became accustomed to sitting through declines. Thus, when the inevitable big break did come, they continued to hold onto their positions.

They had learned one successful policy — buy and hold — only to become strong adherents to that policy at a time when it was imperative to learn a new trading game.

Always ask yourselves, "who has been making the money — and how?" Over any extended period of time, if it's been just the bulls, or just the bears, or just the people working trading ranges, you can bet they've been lulled into thinking that policy will work forever. It won't. The market will do its utmost to get their money back.

Don't let that happen to you. Place stops closely under your long positions; about 1½ limits is ample. The same with your short positions, but about 2 limit moves. Don't be afraid to sell on strong up days — after all, even the strongest markets must correct. When prices begin acting too emotionally, after a large move, be ready to sell on the next strong up day, or cover your shorts on a strong down day.

## THE MOST IMPORTANT TRADING ADVICE I CAN GIVE YOU

Without a doubt, the most important trading advice I can give you is:

**BUY ONLY ON DOWN DAYS**
**SELL ONLY ON UP DAYS**

That advice is worth thousands of dollars. It's hard to follow, like all good market techniques. But, it's dynamite. It will put you into positions at optimum prices where you are protected and well-entrenched.

The herd instinct almost forces us to buy on up days while the laws of probability (which work well with commodities) tell us that up days are more likely to be followed by down days. Especially if it's the third or fourth up day of a move. Don't fall for these sucker plays!

## WHEN TO TAKE YOUR PROFITS

In summary, hold onto your profitable positions with reasonable stops under the market.

Hold on until you are stopped out, or

1. a long term momentum trend line is broken, or

2. blow off action appears.

One of these three profit taking developments will occur. Nothing else can happen. Most often, it will be that you are stopped out as a correction enters the market. That's fine. Then get ready to position yourself for the next major move in the commodity.

Such pull backs and consolidations will last from five to twenty days. Their demise, and the birth of a new trend, will be signaled by %R and/or momentum indices. Should these not click, (they almost always do) chart action will give you your indication of when to get back aboard.

## WHEN TO MOVE STOPS CLOSER

There are a number of developments that may make you want to move your stops closer to the market. One important criteria would be when your cyclical analysis tells you it's about time for the next phase of the cycle to unfold and selling pressures are expected.

Or perhaps it's a new moon, or full moon time. That's an excellent opportunity for a trend reversal and tells us to get those stops close to our profits.

A third opportunity for raising stops would be if the nearby premium begins to disintegrate. Re-read the chapter on premiums and the comments I made about the significance of losing the premium. When this happens it's a certain sign of impending market weakness. Such a signal clearly tells us to get those stops right up there to protect and preserve our capital.

## A CLOSING COMMENT

I have tried to make this a simple little book that explains and discusses the approach and tools I used to make $1,000,000 in the market last year. It is my belief that good books, on any subject, should be concise. What I look for, personally, is performance and facts, and I'm certain that is the way you would like to be dealt with as well.

The concepts, ideas, and tools herein are good — very good. With proper application, and that's the real secret, you can easily make 30% to 100% and more each and every year on your commodity equity.

Please believe me when I say that I have given you all of my secrets. I have held nothing back. It's all right here in print, everything I know about trading commodities. While reader's comments are always appreciated, I do not have the time to respond to all the letters a book of this nature will generate. My phones are unlisted for the same reason. Please allow me my own solitude. I need it for research and trading purposes.

## YOUR SUCCESS

You will only be as successful as you really want to be. If, deep down inside, you want to lose, you'll figure out a way of losing using my system. If you want to win just a little bit, my system will help you to accomplish that. If you want to win big, as I wanted to do, the system can also accomodate you.

I hope you have enjoyed this book as much as I've enjoyed writing it. The ideas expressed herein will be invaluable as long as commodities are traded. All you need now is,

Good luck, and good trading!